Object Lessons

EAVAN BOLAND

Object Lessons

*The Life of the Woman and the Poet
in Our Time*

CARCANET PRESS ◆ MANCHESTER

First published in Great Britain in 1995 by
Carcanet Press Limited
402-406 Corn Exchange Buildings
Manchester M4 3BY

A CIP catalogue record for this book
is available from the British Library.
ISBN 1 85754 074 3

The publisher acknowledges financial
assistance from the Arts Council of England

Printed and bound in England by SRP Ltd, Exeter

Funded by
THE
ARTS
COUNCIL
OF ENGLAND

for my mother,
the friend of my lifetime

I wish to thank the American-Ireland Fund for its Literary Award in 1994, which helped with the time to complete this text.
I wish to note the generosity of the Lannan Foundation in giving me a 1994 Lannan Award for Poetry.

CONTENTS

I began to write in an enclosed, self-confident literary culture. The poet's life stood in a burnished light in the Ireland of that time. Poets were still poor, had little sponsored work and could not depend on a sympathetic reaction to their poetry. But the idea of the poet was honored. It was an emblem to the whole culture that self-expression and survival could combine. A contested emblem, certainly—the relation was never easy and may even, in certain ways, have been corrupt—but it existed, it was there. A poet was remarked upon and pointed out, was sometimes quoted, and the habits and sayings of poets frequently found their way into a sort of image file of idiosyncrasy which further reinforced the sense of poetry as something in high relief and set apart.

A woman's life was not honored. At least no one I knew suggested that it was exemplary in the way a poet's was. As dusk fell in the city, a conversational life intensified. Libraries filled up; the green-cowled lamps went on, and light pooled onto open pages. The pubs were crowded. The cafés were full of students and apprentice writers like myself, some of them talking about literature, a very few talking intensely about poetry.

Only a few miles away was the almost invisible world that everyone knew of and no one referred to. Of suburbs and housing estates. Of children and women. Of fires lighted for the first winter chill; of food put on the table. The so-called ordinary world, which most of us had come from and some would return to on the last bus, was not even mentioned. Young poets are like children. They assume the dangers to themselves are those their elders identified; they internalize the menace without analyzing it. It was not said, it was not even consciously thought and yet I absorbed the sense that poetry was safe here in this city at twilight, with its violet sky and constant drizzle, within this circle of libraries and pubs and talks about stanzas and cadences. Beyond it was the ordinariness which could only dissipate it; beyond it was a life for which no visionary claim could be made.

The opposite is now true. A woman's life—its sexuality,

its ritual, its history—has become a brilliantly lit motif, in-
fluencing the agenda of culture and commerce alike. At the
same time the old construct of the poet's life, for which I have
such an exasperated tenderness, has lost some of the faith and
trust of a society. Increasingly, it is perceived as arcane and
worse: as a code of outdated power systems whose true purpose was to exalt not the poet's capacity to suffer but his suit-
ability for election to a category which made him or her
exempt from the shared experience of others.

◆　◆　◆

I know now that I began writing in a country where the
word *woman* and the word *poet* were almost magnetically opposed. One word was used to invoke collective nurture, the
other to sketch out self-reflective individualism. Both states
were necessary—that much the culture conceded—but they
were oil and water and could not be mixed. It became part of
my working life, part of my discourse, to see these lives evade
and simplify each other. I became used to the flawed space
between them. In a certain sense, I found my poetic voice by
shouting across that distance.

But I was also hostage to it. As a young woman and an
uncertain poet, I wanted there to be no contradiction between the way I made an assonance to fit a line and the way I
lifted up a child at night. But there were many; they were
deep-seated, they inflected arguments of power and pre-
sumption which were obvious to me and yet unexamined in
any critique I knew.

The relative status of these lives has changed. The power of each to limit and smooth out the complexity of the other has not. In the old situation which existed in the Dublin I first knew, it was possible to be a poet, permissible to be a woman and difficult to be both without flouting the damaged and incomplete permissions on which Irish poetry had been constructed.

The new situation has made a role reversal. Now poetry itself, and the concept of the poet, have been put under severe pressure by any number of factors, among which the emergence of women and the new importance ascribed to a woman's life are a real and powerful presence.

Here and throughout this book these lives remain the theme. These, after all, are the two lives—a woman's and a poet's—that I have lived and understood. They are the lives whose aspirations I honor, and they remain divided. I have written freely about both, and sometimes my pen has skidded on the modest particulars. I am not a scholar, and my historical sense is selective. My working life has been spent not in any aspiration towards knowledge or accuracy but in an intuitive struggle with form. And yet at certain points in writing this book, I have caught a glimpse of the wider implications of the theme. At these moments it has seemed to me that these lives, with their relation and division, make a sign which is ominous and revealing: about silence and expression, about democratization and oligarchy, about the life a society tolerates and the one it nominates to take it into the future, to both glory and survival.

II.

I have put this book together not as a prose narrative is usually constructed but as a poem might be: in turnings and returnings. In parts which find and repeat themselves and restate the argument until it loses its reasonable edge and hopefully becomes a sort of cadence. Therefore, the reader will come on the same room more than once: the same tablecloth with red-checked squares; the identical table by an open window. An ordinary suburb, drenched in winter rain, will show itself once, twice, then disappear and come back. The Dublin hills will change color in the distance, and change once more. The same October day will happen, as it never can in real life, over and over again.

In various pieces I have returned to the same themes and their interpretation, often to the exact room and the identical moment in the suburb when the light goes out of the sky and dusk comes. I will need the reader's patience as, once again, I go back to the visionary place, the obstructed moment. Not so much because of an aspiration to give a definite shape to the book but because each revisiting has offered me another chance to clarify the mystery of being a poet in the puzzle of time and sexuality and nationhood.

Argument and recollection may not solve the puzzle, but they have allowed me to note it. They have also allowed me to make a record of the interior of the poem as I found it; its angles of relation to my life and circumstance. There is nothing definitive about this; such angles are subjectively observed and understood. But it is also true that they are not found in textbooks, at least not for a working poet. They are best seen where they have most effect: at the actual moment of writing a poem.

And in a sense it is the very smallness of this moment and the ordinary furnishings which surround it—a suburban dusk, a table by an open window with a book and a pen on it—which have led me to a larger contention. To make it at all clearly here, as against the diffused form in which it appears throughout this book, I will have to return to the argument.

In an odd and poignant way these two lives, of a poet and a woman, have proved to be formidable historical editors of each other. In previous centuries, when the poet's life was an emblem for the grace and power of a society, a woman's life was often the object of his expression: in pastoral, sonnet, elegy. As the mute object of his eloquence her life could be at once addressed and silenced. By an ironic reversal, now that a woman's life is that emblem of grace and power, the democratization of our communities, of which her emergence is one aspect, makes a poet's life look suspect, can make it appear, to a wider society, elite and irrelevant all at once. Therefore, for anyone who is drawn into either of these lives, the pressure is there to betray the other: to disown or simplify, to resolve an inherent tension by making a false design from the ethical capabilities of one life or the visionary possibilities of the other.

It is these very tensions, and not their absence, and not

any possibility of resolving them, which makes me believe that the woman poet is now an emblematic figure in poetry, much as the modernist or romantic poets were in their time. I make this less as a claim than as a historical reading. It does not mean she will write better poetry than men, or more important or more lasting. It does mean that in the projects she chooses, must choose perhaps, are internalized some of the central stresses and truths of poetry at this moment. And that in the questions she needs to ask herself—about voice and self, about revising the stance of the poet, not to mention the relation of the poem to the act of power—are some of the questions which are at the heart of the contemporary form. This does not give her any special liberty to subcontract a poem to an ideology. It does not set her free to demand that a bad poem be reconsidered as a good ethic. Her responsibilities remain the same as they have been for every poet: to formalize the truth. At the same time the advantage she gains for language, the clarities she brings to the form, can no longer be construed as sectional gains. They must be seen as pertaining to all poetry. That means they must also be allowed access to that inner sanctum of a tradition: its past.

At the age of seventeen I left school. I went to university, and I wrote my first attempts at poetry in a room in a flat at the edge of the city. That room appears often in this book. I can see it now, and I have wanted the reader to see it. It was not large. It looked north rather than south. The window beside the table was small and inclined to stick on rainy afternoons. And yet for me, as for so many other writers in so many other rooms, this particular one remains a place of origin.

But one thing was lacking. There were times when I sat down at that table, or came up the stairs, my key in my hand, to open the door well after midnight, when I missed something. I wanted a story. I wanted to read or hear the narrative of someone else—a woman and a poet—who had gone here, and been there. Who had lifted a kettle to a gas stove. Who had set her skirt out over a chair, near to the clothes dryer, to have it without creases for the morning. Who had made the life meet the work and had set it down: the difficulties and rewards; the senses of lack. I remember thinking that it need not be perfect or important. Just there; just available. And I have remembered that.

PART ONE

Objects

1.

In the early days of October, in the year 1909, a woman entered a Dublin hospital, near the center of the city. The building is still there. If you approach from the south, with the Dublin hills behind you, and look down a tunnel of grace made by the houses of Fitzwilliam and Merrion squares, your view will end abruptly in this: the National Maternity Hospital, red brick and out of character, blocking the vista. The rooms inside are functional and light-eating. They show no evidence of that zest for air and proportion which was the mask of an Augustan oppressor.

October is a beautiful month in the city. If you turn around and go back towards the hills, away from the hospital, the roads are narrow and gracious above the canal. The woman who entered the hospital may have passed them as she made her way to it. If, for instance, she drove around Stephen's Green, having arrived on the late-morning train from Drogheda, she may also have noticed a trick of light peculiar to that time of year: In the dark corridor of Lower Leeson Street, sunlight cuts the houses in half. Halfway up the brick, the reflection of the houses opposite builds another street: chimneys, roofs, gutters made of unglittering shadow.

She may not have come that way. She might have traveled down the unglamorous back streets that lead more directly to the hospital. Fenian Street. Hogan Place. Past the mills. Past the Dodder River on its way to the Liffey. Up the slight gradient which would still, in that year, be cobbled. The prewinter chill, which can be felt on some October mornings, could have struck extra music out of the horses' hooves.

It is not a long drive. But whatever she saw that morning, it is lost. Whatever that journey yielded—the child with a hoop who never existed, the woman with a red hat I am now inventing—they were her last glimpses of the outside world.

◆ ◆ ◆

This is the way we make the past. This is the way I will make it here. Listening for hooves. Glimpsing the red hat which was never there in the first place. Giving eyesight and evidence to a woman we never knew and cannot now recover. And for all our violations, the past waits for us. The road from the train to the hospital opens out over and over again, vacant and glittering, offering shadows and hats and hoops. Again and again I visit it and reinvent it. But the woman who actually traveled it had no such license. Hers was a real journey. She did not come back. On October 10 she died in the National Maternity Hospital. She was thirty-one years of age. She was my grandmother.

◆ ◆ ◆

Nineteen hundred and nine. It was a different city and another time. The difference is worth settling on. The following year George Roberts of Maunsel and Co., the Dublin publishing house, would write to James Joyce promising him the proofs of "Ivy Day in the Committee Room." The proofs would not arrive. A little later Roberts would write again. He would ask Joyce to remove all references to the king in his story. Towards the end of 1910 Augustine Birrell would inform William Butler Yeats that his civil list pension, at last, could be counted on. "I know you don't care about Doctor Johnson," he wrote, "but I always think his pension was the money best spent in England during the whole of my beloved eighteenth century. It is well that the Twentieth should follow suit."

5

It was a year on the edge of political upheaval. In the next fourteen months England would have two general elections. The second one yielded a result which was important for Ireland. True enough, only 84 out of 272 successful Liberal candidates so much as mentioned Home Rule in their election addresses. Nevertheless, as the results were gradually declared throughout December 1910, it became clear that the Liberals would depend for their majority in the House of Commons on the Irish members there. It was also clear that the driven, ambitious son of a Yorkshire wool manufacturer had changed his mind. Herbert Asquith, now prime minister of England, who had once vowed the Liberal party would never take office again if they were to depend on the Irish members, now accepted the result. Unlike other politicians of the time, his literacy extended to the writing on the wall. In April 1912, by introducing the Third Home Rule Bill, he would set tar barrels and bonfires blazing throughout Ireland.

The city which waited upon these changes was itself changing. In 1909 it was a place of approximately a quarter of a million souls. We have to imagine a town of bowler hats, bicycles, trams and red uniforms. By all contemporary accounts, it was a mixture of occupation and indigenous obstinacy. There were frequent recruiting marches for the British army. New recruits, after all, got a shilling there and then—an amount hard to resist. The police still chased thieves and arrested drunks while wearing the uniform of the Royal Irish Constabulary. Horses were everywhere. James Joyce would repeat the city superstition that you never crossed O'Connell

Bridge without seeing a white horse. Bystanders tell of the small daily theater of watching runaway horses break out of the shafts and even, on occasion, collide into shopfronts. On the corner of Marlborough Street there was a shop which sold pigs' trotters in brown paper bags.

Poverty was widespread. The death rate for Dublin was the highest of any city in Europe. In Britain Street and Gardiner Street and Rutland Street, all north of the Liffey, evictions were a daily occurrence. Trade unionists blamed the bad housing and worse health conditions on a corrupt city council, mainly of Irish nationalists.

A place on the edge. A place of resentment and beauty and conflict. All abstract qualities perhaps, but nonetheless potent for that. In another ten years it would all change again. There would be gunfire in these streets and outside the windows of the building she died in. There would be carts and lorries full of hostages carried to and fro by the Black and Tans. The glittering dances, the genteel imitations of British manners practiced by those who saw no tomorrow in this year of 1909 would be waning ten years from now. The schemes and conspiracies of those who could not tolerate the present moment—the men and women with the "vivid faces" Yeats referred to in his poem—would soon be vindicated.

♦ ♦ ♦

How much did she care? Politics and social change, except as it touched her immediate circumstances, could only

have seemed a distant drum. The facts of her life are briefly
stated; none of them makes an obvious intersection with political change. She came from a large family. She lived in the
midlands of Ireland. She married a seaman in her late teens.
He became a master mariner and then a sea captain. She had
five daughters. She died in a Dublin hospital.

Even the fact that she was the wife of a seagoing husband
put her at a remove from some of the most intense national
questions. In 1903, for instance, George Wyndham, the chief
secretary for Ireland, managed to pass a new Land Purchase
Act in the House of Commons. It was easily the most satisfac-
tory settlement yet of the festering question of British landlor-
dism. She and her husband lived in a cottage on the outskirts
of Drogheda. I have no doubt it was rented. If they had been
tenant farmers instead, living on the estates whose demesne
walls ran from one end of Ireland to the other, she would
have noticed the change. By a clause in the act, tenants could
now buy their lands and the legal cost of transfer would be
met from public funds. This was a new and attractive provi-
sion. Landlords benefited also. If a whole estate was sold, they
were rewarded with a 12 percent bonus on top of the purchase price. In another six years 270,000 land purchases had
been negotiated out of a possible half million tenant occupa-
tions. And she was dying.

◆ ◆ ◆

A hundred years ago she was a child. But where? Strange
to think that once the circumstances of her life were simple

8

and available. They have become, with time, fragments and guesswork.

I have pieces, but they are few enough. But she has a name. Three names, in fact. Mary Ann Sheils. There is a faint surprise about the three flat take-it-or-leave-it syllables of the Christian names. Mary Ann sounds more like the name of a younger sister in a Jane Austen novel than a girl from the end of the nineteenth century in Ireland. Then again, it was a time of turmoil, and turmoil is easily negotiated into ambivalence. Which in turn can be seen in the Irish endowing their sons and daughters with echoes of the names given to the children of squires and vicars across the water.

I know nothing about her childhood. There are no photographs. No letters. Nobody ever recalled her to me as living memory. It is another erasure. And yet something does survive: a story so odd and strange that it has the power to upstage all those icons and arrangements that survive the re-corded childhoods of official family histories. It is a story I heard twice—so improbable that each time I thought of it as one of those signs the past makes when it has transferred its available resources from memory to allegory.

♦ ♦ ♦

She came from a family of millers. Sometime after the famine they left the small fishing town of Milford in Donegal. Hard pressed as they were, they must still have missed the idiosyncrasy of their own place: the sight of Mulroy Bay in February light. The main street with its steep climb up the side of a hill. They moved east and south to the town of Dundalk. There the business failed. And they moved again to Leitrim, where her father was born. It was to him that legend clung. And the way I build that legend now is the way I heard it: out of rumor, fossil fact, half memories.

He was a small man, compact and saturnine in the way of many western people. If he was anything like his son, whom I met for a few hours years ago, he had eloquent and strained features. A fine profile. Close-set, obstinate eyes. There was something strained and pinched about it all which kept it well away from beauty. He grew up in Leitrim, and sometime in his early manhood—I imagine the early 1870s— he had fallen in love with a local girl. I know so little about her or him that I must become the fictional interventionist here and say that she was, of course, winning and expressive and utterly true to him. And that he loved her stubbornly.

But there was an obstacle. She was a younger sister. In the manner of fairy tales, her older sister was plain and deserving and on no account to be slighted by having the younger girl marry first.

And so it went around. The parents insisted he should offer his suit to the older sister. They may have offered him inducements, but I doubt it. The inducement can only have been local custom and iron decorum. There were no dowries. These were poor people, reduced in circumstance by a difficult century, utterly vulnerable to the sickness of a heifer or a farthing's change in the price of wheat. They would have brought to bear on him the influence of local opinion and approval. He must marry the older girl, and that was that. He was implacable. It would be the younger one, and that was all. The younger girl retained her love for him, and he for her. Finally—and now the narrative quickens, gets unsteady, fills with unknown passages of time and event—the impasse yielded. Love triumphed. The wedding day was set.

I have no document or certificate. I have Mary Ann's marriage certificate but not this one. In any case, the cold signatures of the witnesses and the sacristan could do no justice to the event. The wedding day came. It seems safe to imagine a small granite church in the middle of a townland and the weather, more than likely, gray and overcast. Perhaps the turnout was a bit more than usual because of the notoriety of the whole thing; the struggle of wills and all the gossip and curiosity incurred on that account. The bride came, dressed in white and heavily veiled. The vows were taken and repeated, said by the bride and the groom. The priest pronounced them man and wife. For a single moment it must have seemed to him that some wound of ill luck and misadventure in his own life had undergone a miraculous healing.

Then he lifted her veil. But it was not—the story turns gothic now—the face he loved. Convention had prevailed. The family had smuggled in the older, plainer girl, and he was bound to her by iron convention and legality for the rest of his life.

◆ ◆ ◆

The nineteenth century, especially the second half of it, was a time of restatement in Ireland. After the famine, after the failed rebellions of the forties and sixties, the cultural and political desires for self-determination began to shape each other in a series of riffs on independence and identity. It was an exciting time but not a pure one. Self-consciousness mixed in with improvisation, and not always happily. A new interest in the language and customs of Ireland went hand in hand with instinctive, colonial attempts to metabolize that interest into something weaker and less threatening. The love of a nation is a particularly dangerous thing when the nation predates the state. The danger was partly handled by a tabloid version of it, which suited British drawing rooms and did not put an obvious sell-by-date on empire.

From this confused time come the false and synthetic Irish dances, the suspect emblems of harps and Celtic crosses. And while the Fenians experimented with real terror, the drawing-room version of Irish nationalism became acceptable and even fashionable. A genteel mix of nostalgia and sentiment.

This was the time when legends began to be dignified as myths. Cuchulain. The Red Branch Knights. Maeve. Conchubar. They reemerged from a lost scholarly past, but in the shape of a Victorian Round Table. While hayricks burned and gunfire could be heard at night after evictions, Germanic scholars worked over the old Irish stories and resurrected them in a new European time frame.

In all this some of the real myths were ignored: those

down-to-earth and hand-to-mouth yarns which start in fear
and short-circuit into a pure and elaborate invention. Which
bind a community together not by what they explain but by
the very fact that they were forced to explain it. I can only
think this must be one of them, this Rachel and Leah fable
about beauty and denial. It is a wonderful image for something: a man lifting a veil on a plain and peremptory face. But
for what? For history? For fate?

To me—the great-granddaughter whose existence was
guaranteed when his was cheated—it seems to be something
else. I think of it as the Gothic yearning to find for random
misfortune something approaching the ritual and astonish-
ment of the coffins certain enclosed orders lie down and sleep
in at night, something which dignifies horror by anticipating
it. He was an unlucky man. He had an unlucky daughter.

His vows finished on that lost day, in that small church,
before curious neighbors, he accepted his lot and took his
wife to his bed. They had thirteen children. It hardly seems an
elegy for lost love. Six of those children survived. Mary Ann
was one of them.

He died in the asylum in Mullingar. Of mental illness.
Or drink. Or that combination of both which in Ireland, as
anywhere else, might just cover a broken heart.

◆ ◆ ◆

This is not a story about luck, or even memory, but
about what replaces them. And whether we have the right to
replace them. She survived, but only in fits and starts of oral

recollection and memory. Looking back, I can see those fractions, those chances more clearly.

I left school when I was seventeen. A rainy summer in-
tervened before I began my courses at Trinity College. Sometime during these months my mother showed me the only
piece of paper—a letter from her father to her mother—in her
possession. It was an unusual act. Unlike most people, she
treated the past as an opportunity for forgetfulness rather than
a source of definition. She had no photographs, not one, of
herself as a child. No copybooks from school. No pantomime
tickets. She talked of her childhood rarely and without sentiment. Almost, it seemed, without interest.

I understand this better now than I used to. There are
parts of Europe, and commentators like Claudio Magris are
witnesses to it, where minorities, even nations, jostle in the
same square mile. Change a language, turn a signpost, rename
a village, and the previous identity becomes a figment, a hostage to persistence and stubborn recall. Magris speaks of a
woman describing the country she loves, "which like all
motherlands," he states, "exists perhaps only in this love."
My mother wanted to forget. Childhood was a place of un-
readable signposts and overgrown roads. The language could
not be retrieved.

I took the letter from her in the back room of the flat I
shared with my sisters. I bent my head to read it. My grandfather had written it at sea; there were references to the weather
and the voyage. The handwriting was clear and sloping, and
the pages were lined. The garden, with its path to a locked

wooden door, stayed at the upper edge of my sight. I was
conscious of fruit trees and the chicken wire at the base of
them. When that splintered door was unlocked, it opened
onto a towpath and the urban containment of the river Dodder. When you stood there, in the occasional July sunshine,
you had a view of a stone wall, trees. You could hear cars and
buses. You could see the roofs shelving into the city where
she died. Now that landscape faltered. The North Sea raised
its gray wall and swell outside the window.

The address at the start of the letter was declamatory,
affectionate. My dearest wife? My darling wife? Then there
were two things which I remember even now. The first was
just a housekeeping detail. It made reference to a collection
on board for one of the ship's mates. For a hardship, perhaps,
or a gift or a leave-taking. In any case, the tone of the account
is apologetic. He had given a half crown. Two shillings and
sixpence in old money. It was a good amount, he knew, but
he felt constrained to do it. He felt she would understand.

A fraction indeed. Even so, the door opens a crack. I see
her more clearly. She must have had three children by now,
maybe four, and one was sickly. Milk. Rent. Doctor's bills.
Clothes. Every penny counted. A sea captain made respectable money, relative to the unrest and uncertainty in Ireland
at that time. But the distances must have made it seem at risk,
and all the more important that as much salary as possible
returned home intact.

The second detail is clearer. There is a yearning note in
the letter. The small talk of money and clothes—I remember

some mention of a singlet—is anxious rather than anecdotal. The intimacy is of someone trying to set up house between Drogheda and the North Sea. Then the words I remember most clearly, although not exactly or in sequence. This is a paraphrase: "I don't know why I always fear that something bad will happen, but I do."

It is not a passionate letter. It is an anxious and domestic one, and yet I am certain theirs was a passionate marriage. One detail supports that view. It was repeated to and remembered by my mother. It is the sort of small vignette which is extravagant, and enough out of character with the penny-wise young mother, to be repeated and remembered. Whenever my grandfather's ship docked, often at Cork Harbor, Mary Ann would go and meet him. She did this because she feared the women at the ports.

II.

How do we create such figures? What act of love or corruption makes us turn to a past full of obstruction and misinformation? I am forty-nine years of age. She has been there all my life, a maquette of fables and possibilities. And yet at a certain point she ceased to be merely a suggestion and became a presence. In that sense, her story is mine also. Where exactly did I discover her? Or, more precisely, when?

♦ ♦ ♦

This at least I can be fairly certain of. In my thirties I found myself, to use a colloquial fiction, in a suburban house

16

at the foothills of the Dublin mountains. Married and with
two little daughters. I led a life which would have been recognizable to any woman who had led it and to many others who
had not. My days were arrayed with custom and necessity,
acts so small their momentousness was visible to nobody but
myself. Season by season I separated cotton from wool and
the bright digits of gloves from ankle socks. I drove the car. I
collected children from school. In spring the petals from
across the road blew down, strewing the curbs with the impression of a summer wedding. In February, after a high
wind, the village street was littered with slates.

But at night the outer landscape yielded to an inner one.
Familiar items blanked out and were replaced by others. The
streetlamp stood in for the whitebeam tree; the planet of rain
around it displaced the rowanberries. And in those darknesses
I lay down as conscious of love for my children as I would
have been of a sudden and chartless fever. And conscious also
of how that love spread out from the bed on which I lay, and
out further to the poplar trees, to the orange plastic mug at
one side of the hedge, to the glint of a bicycle wheel and the
half-moon.

I understood then, as any human being would, the difference between love and a love which is visionary. The first
may well be guaranteed by security and attachment; only the
second has the power to transform. As I lay there, my mind
went seeking well beyond the down-to-earth and practical
meaning of a daily love. The apple trees. The rustle and click
of shadow leaves. The mysterious cycle of plants. In those

17

darknesses it could seem to me that this was not a world in which my love happened but one whose phenomena occurred because of it.

Poetry is full of such transformations. They are, for example, the weather of most love poems. They constitute much of the perspective of the great conventions, such as the pastoral. I ought to have felt that my experiences, even my half-formed impressions at this time, connected well with my training as a poet. But I did not. As each morning came around, with its fresh sights and senses, I felt increasingly the distance between my own life, my lived experience and conventional interpretations of both poetry and the poet's life. It was not exactly or even chiefly that the recurrences of my world—a child's face, the dial of a washing machine—were absent from the tradition, although they were. It was not even so much that I was a woman. It was that being a woman, I had entered into a life for which poetry has no name.

◆ ◆ ◆

Names. Every art is inscribed with them. Every life depends on them. I was to find out, as I searched for information about her, just how wounding their absence can be.

I knew that she was buried in a small graveyard outside Drogheda, in the village of Termonfeckin. I drove there one Saturday, on the very edge of the month in which she died. September is a time of mild weather in Ireland. Great swatches of light are draped across stone and fields; there is a misleading stillness. October is different. The zone between the two months can seem to be a season in itself, an emblematic journey from fruition to menace.

I drove out by North Dublin. Beyond Swords is the small seaside village of Rush, with its fine strands and the potato farms which supply the Dublin markets. Then Balbriggan, with its old cotton factory. Then fields with great cylinders of saved hay. Past here the road follows the Boyne estuary into Drogheda.

It was a wild afternoon with a clay-and-mortar sky. Heavy rains the night before had left the Boyne churning. I drove over the bridge into Drogheda, into a town crowded with Saturday afternoon shoppers. I drove up one hill and down the next, then followed a sign into a quiet street.

She must have lived, I thought, somewhere along this road. The distance between Drogheda and Termonfeckin is a brief five or six miles. In her time it must have seemed much longer. Over the century the town had extended so that at least half the road between the two was taken up with front gardens and bungalows. A school. A post office. Petrol stations and newsagents.

After a few miles, however, it is all rural again. Sycamores and ivy-choked oaks block the roadside. The ditches are full of dead branches and cow parsley. As I started the approach to Termonfeckin, I was halted by a small herd of black and white cows, a harlequin back view of haunches. Two boys and a girl were herding them, gesturing and laughing. I slowed down between towns, between centuries. The queue of cars behind me lengthened. Then a gate opened into a field. I heard a sound of voices, more laughter. The road was clear again.

◆ ◆ ◆

Termonfeckin lies in a flat landscape between Clogher Head to the northeast and the estuary of the Boyne to the south. As I drove in, I had a ghost impression of the Surrey villages of my childhood. A self-possessed quietness. A dignified slope of ivy-colored walls and slated roofs. Trees and gates and high, well-trimmed hedges. It is a small town, with a population of a few thousand at most. And yet its history is entrenched and visible. Until the seventeenth century the archbishops of Armagh had their summer residence here. The name itself is an abbreviation of the Irish. *Tearmann Feichin.* St. Feichin's sanctuary land.

She must have lived within striking distance of this village. This is not a deduction so much as simple fact. In Ireland, as elsewhere, it is customary that people are christened and married and buried in the parish in which they are born or wed or die. Not an invariable custom perhaps but a reliable one all the same. She must have kept together her small family of girls within reach of these trees and slopes, perhaps only a mile or so away. She would have known this village with its steep, leafy roads and its rural peace.

The graveyard is on the edge of the town, up a small gradient so steep and narrow that only one car can fit with any safety. It takes two or three minutes to drive there, but with every one of them the shade deepens, the trees seem to darken. Then finally there is a widening out, a quadrangle of grass bounded at one end by an ornate iron gate. On the other side of it are a church steeple and, beyond, a clear view to the Boyne estuary. The church is not especially old. A date of 1904 is above the lintel.

The gate was closed but not locked. Once inside, I could see that the graveyard shelved out above fields and some houses. Two graveyards, to be accurate. One on either side of the church. It was as if the church were flanked by two separate plots, neither of them much bigger than a small back garden. To the left of the steeple there was the appearance of a normal graveyard: polished slate and marble, important lettering, recent flowers and some plastic ones. To the right was a plot which seemed to come from another century, another ethos. Even the grass seemed more unkempt, and the whole appearance was of a small field of old and often broken headstones. No granite, no marble. Only stone and very little of it that could be clearly read. One of the best of the headstones was still cracked diagonally, as if with an arrow through a heart in a child's drawing. The inscription read: "Erected by Widow Rodgers of Parsonstown in memory of her beloved husband Edward who departed this life June 1818."

In the cold afternoon these words seemed to me to have an extravagant dignity. Just the name, the language, the location of a human life in the remembrance of it. What was pitiful all around it were the small clumps of stone, giants' handfuls of granite, tossed around, apparently at random. Occasionally one of these had a name, cut roughly into its surface and thoroughly worn. Most of them did not.

Less than a hundred years after that inscription her coffin had been brought here. Through these iron gates and onto the raised shelf of this ground. None of the scattered pieces of granite was bigger than a man's head. None was polished or even shaped. I began to search through them for her name, reaching my hand down through high grass and moss as if into water, trying to feel a lettering. More often than not there was none. The stones were rough; not one was polished or even shaped. Yet in the heartbroken vernacular of the place, each one stood in for a life, a death.

The wind was suddenly bitter. I had a sense of anomaly and intrusion. Just below the graveyard there was a bungalow, with its garden at right angles to the church. Two dogs, one brown and one black, regarded me seriously: a woman in a raincoat, stooping and searching. It seemed of enormous, irrational importance that I should find her name. Her name, carved against the odds into one of those wretched stone markers. I tried to imagine her funeral as I searched: desolate October weather, the hurried retrieval of her body from a Dublin hospital. And what, if any of this, could the discovery of her name offset? I found other names. Sometimes just initials, sometimes a full Christian name. But not hers.

I was astonished at how much I felt the small, abstract wound. A woman I had never met and never seen. A woman my mother could only have seen in a period of days or weeks which left no memory. Yet the indignity of her aftermath at this moment in this graveyard was one of the worst parts of her story. Five children. A life of work. A husband whose language had some grace of love and concern about it, even across distance. I was certain, in some more rational part of my mind, that her headstone was indeed here. She had been too much loved and noted for it not to have been. But the fact was I could not find it. Somehow that temporary confusion had become in this dull light a sign for a wider loss. She had turned her head for it, come running to it as a child, hoped for it on a letter and answered it in moments of love. And now she had no memorial because she had no name.

III.

Was there really no name for my life in poetry? The question preoccupied me more as time went on. And if not, why not? War poetry. Nature poetry. Love poetry. Pastoral poetry. The comic epic. The tragic lyric. Surely there were names enough there for any and every life. Even if the name of my experience, of what I felt and saw, was not specifically entered there, then why not represent my life as one which those conventions, those traditions could name and therefore recognize? In theory it could be done and had been done. As I walked between the whitebeams on my way to call the children home on a summer evening, I was all too aware of how a nuance here and a shadow there could turn me into a woman already recognized by and therefore recognizable to poetic convention.

The way to the past is never smooth. For a woman poet

it can be especially tortuous. Every step towards an origin is also an advance towards a silence. The past in which our grandmothers lived and where their lives burned through detail and daily incidence to become icons for our future is also a place where women and poetry remain far apart. What troubles me is not how difficult and deceptive my relation to this past—and to this figure within it—may be but that it might not have existed at all.

I began writing poetry at a time when, and in a tradition where, poetry appeared to be granted authentic communal importance. I learned, although not quickly, that such grants are provisory and conditional. The mystique was sustained by prescriptions. Poetry, it was suggested, was something of power and resonance. It was also a good deal removed from that life which was deemed ordinary. Therefore, I began in a poetic world where the names were so established, so imposing and powerful it never occurred to me they might not be equally inclusive. I read Yeats first when I was sixteen. There was a small room in the boarding school where I was a pupil. The window sloped at right angles to the ceiling and looked out on grass and a eucalyptus tree and the Irish Sea glittering through evergreens. Early in the morning the acoustics of water and altitude made the sound of a church bell pure and astonishing.

I read Yeats's poetry in that room. In the morning before classes began. And again at night, under thick blankets and with a flashlamp. I took in, with some kind of recognition, and through the gestures of language, exciting and powerful statements. I did not know enough about what he was doing to identify the enterprise. Later I would know the barriers he had broken: In the dark corridor between the fin-de-siècle and modernism he had found a door and opened it. To the question of whether the poetic self is created or invented he had given a poignant and effective answer: both.

But there were aspects of that reading which troubled me. It began as a small doubt and widened, in my twenties and thirties, into a pervasive sense of unease. Yes, his best poems showed him nameless and powerless before old age and approaching death. But he had moved to that position from solid recognitions. Before he even lifted his pen, his life awaited him in poetry. He was Irish. A man. A nationalist. A disappointed lover. Even his aging was recorded. The values were set. I was to learn how hard it would be to set different values.

From then on I read poetry eagerly. In college my experience of it widened. Some images remained long after I had closed the book: Keats's Hyperion. His starry tantrum on the edges of day and night. Gawain riding through frozen countryside. Only gradually did I become aware of some kind of paradox slowly developing within this process. That the effect of good poetry—the acute sense of liberation which a command of language and technique brought to me—was offset by a growing sense of oppression. And in all that reading, propping the book up against table or bed, I know now I was not only taking in beauties of phrase but also looking for my name. And it was not there.

25

By the time I left college I knew—it sounds something I should have known much earlier—that I had a mind and a body. That my body would lead my poetry in one direction. That my mind could take up the subtle permissions around me and write a disembodied verse, the more apparently exciting because it denied the existence of the body and that complexity. I knew, in other words, that I was a half-named poet. My mind, my language, my love for freedom: these were named. My body, my instincts: these were named only as passive parts of the poem. Two parts of the poem awaited me. Two choices. Power or powerlessness.

The truth is I began reading and writing poetry in a world where a woman's body was at a safe distance, was a motif and not a menace. For a while I felt sheltered by that. As I read the accepted masters of the tradition, it was all too easy to internalize a sense of power and control. To mistake a command of expression for a resolution of feeling. Such poets handled the feminine image in a way which made the action expressive while the image was silent and passive. At first I saw nothing wrong with that. I was young. I was growing out of my teens in a literary city. I was walking through Stephen's Green on my way to Trinity College, through flowers and water and ducklings, and by the very grass Yeats had walked on where, as my father once told me, he had been behind him and observed that one of his feet turned in. In Newman

House, on the south side of the Green, where I occasionally met friends from the other university, was the room which Joyce described in the tundish chapter of the *Portrait of the Artist.* Literature, it seemed, could have an intimate and even an inherited feel to it.

Everywhere, at least to my eyes, there were signs of the command and ascendancy of poetry. Almost nowhere, at the beginning, did I see its exclusions. Nor did I want to. The exhilaration of language—this is particularly true for a young poet—is almost inseparable from its power. Later the suspect nature of the power would undermine the exhilaration. But not yet.

◆ ◆ ◆

It may well be that women poets of another generation may not feel these things. And yet I do not think it was purely a temporal moment which made me feel as I did; it went deeper. I suspect there will be women again who feel, as I did, that through the act of writing a poem, they have blundered into an ancient world of customs and permissions. That world was The Poem. In it women—their bodies, their existences—had been for thousands of years observed through the active lens of the poem. They had been metaphors and invocations, similes and muses. It had been done not by malice or misogyny but by an encounter between the power of poetic language and the erotic objectifications poetry allowed and encouraged. Custom, convention, language, inherited

27

image: They had all led to the intense passivity of the feminine within the poem. And to this moment when I found my
poetry and my sexuality on a collision course.

For the fact was, in my early twenties, as I bent to write
poems in a copybook on a summer evening, I was entering
upon a subtle and inescapable crisis. I could write lines on the
page. I could type and revise them. I could read them over
again and publish them. I could go through the motions and
act out the role of every young poet. But I felt an estrangement. I had no words for it, and yet I felt it more and more.
Put in the language of hindsight and rationalization, the crisis
was this: However much my powers of expression made my
mind as a human being the subject of the poem, my life as a
woman remained obdurately the object of it.

This was not only bearable while I was a student; it was
hardly noticeable. I was young and ambitious. I wanted to
learn the craft, and I thought in the usual simplifications: that
what was perceived could be learned, that what was learned
could be expressed. The syllogism began to break down the
more I realized that my body was leading me towards a life for
which there was no title and no authorization in the art I had
tried to learn, only an intense and customary passivity. I was a
poet. But I was about to take on the life of the poetic object.
I had written poems. Now I would have to enter them.

Soon enough I was getting married, leaving the flat. I
was about to live a life unrecorded in the tradition I had inherited—in a suburb, with bus timetables and painted shelves
and school runs. I was packing my bookcases, putting my

books in boxes, wrapping my mugs in newspaper and walking back into the poem to be an ancient and component part
of it. A subject silence. The crisis was upon me. I would write
poems. My life would threaten to stay outside them. Half of
me would be in sunlight and half in shadow.

The only resolution of the crisis was both drastic and
isolating. I would have to reexamine modes of expression and
poetic organization that I was, in many ways, accustomed to
and, until then at least, reconciled to. I would have to reexamine and disrupt and dispossess. Not because of feminism,
not because of ideology, but because of poetry.

IV.

Here is her name. Written in a sloping, florid hand
across her death certificate, the letters of the name thick and
thin by turns, where the calligraphic nib pressed down and
eased up. It is a wretched document. What else could it be? It
describes the death of a young woman, far from her home, far
from the sweet chills of a Louth autumn. The National Maternity Hospital was not a natural place for her. She could
only have come there in some out-of-the-ordinary way.
With disease or fever. The cause of death—peritonitis—is
consistent with a complication of puerperal fever, which that
year had swept the lying-in wards of the city. If she did not
have it when she entered the hospital, she was likely to get it
during her stay.

The death certificate I have is simply a copy of page 539
in the registrar's book for the year 1909. Legally she died in

the district of the South Dublin Union. Officially her death was registered there. In the margin it is numbered 453. The page spreads across in a chilling grid: eight checkerboard squares. Name and place of death. Certified cause of death. Age last birthday. And, most bitterly, qualification and residence of informant. In other words, the witness of her death was simply an inmate, S. Murphy, and the address is given as Holles Street. In plain language, my grandmother had died alone, in pain, away from her children and her husband and in a public ward. What she may have feared most and tried to protect against by a small, helpless deception had happened anyway.

◆ ◆ ◆

An unlucky child. Born to an unlucky man. And in a country and a century singularly devoid of that precious substance. One final, small anecdote makes me think she knew it. Or at least had that sort of dread which amounts almost to knowledge.

Her last child was born at midnight. There can hardly have been any excitement about it. This was a fifth child and a fifth girl at that. In those days children were born at home. A midwife would come to the house. In some cases she would stay for two weeks, on either side of the birth.

I wonder how midnight was determined in that house. By a watch? By a striking clock? It must have been the clock, and those imagined chimes ringing through the damp of the house, against the closed windows, around the chintzes and stuffed cushions of the cottage, have everything to do with this story. My mother was born at five minutes to midnight on February 13, 1908. It can be a harsh month in Ireland. Drogheda, with its north-facing aspect, can have frost and even snow at that time. The snowdrops are finished, and the daffodils can already be clumped under rowans and oaks on the roadside. The Boyne will be thick with mist in the early morning.

A baby cried. Five minutes later the clock struck midnight. For the first twenty years of her life my mother believed she had been born on February 14 and held her birthday on that date.

I can almost see those rooms. Somewhere in my childhood the tufts and velvets, the antimacassars and worn textures of Victorianism became as distinct as memory. I came to be aware that my mother hated those colors, those maroons and greens that ate daylight and seemed to be in mourning for themselves.

In those rooms a child was born and a clock chimed. Years later my mother's uncle mentioned to her in passing that one of those five children—he couldn't be sure which—had been born on February 13 at five minutes to midnight. And so superstitious was his sister that she changed the birthday and would only allow it to be on the fourteenth.

A woman full of dread, claiming a sanctuary in superstition which, in the end, circumstance would not allow her. Willing to exchange a child's birthday for a small fiction of safety. Like so much else in this story, it has more than pathos for me. It has that quality of insult which an unchangeable past throws at the present. For my mother, hearing it at twenty, it was old news. She changed her birthday to the right date. By then it was too late for superstition.

v.

I began this piece to make a record of a woman lost in circumstance, a text ironically erased at a time when and in a country where the text was just beginning to be written. I have accepted that the story of Irish history is not her story. The monster rallies, the oil-lit rooms, the flushed faces of orators and the pale ones of assassins have no place in it. Inasmuch as her adult life had a landscape, it was made of the water her husband sailed on and not the fractured, much-claimed piece of earth she was born to.

What was her story? The worst of it is I am not sure. No matter how poignant the details, the narrative is pieced together by something which may itself be a distortion: my own wish to make something orderly out of these fragments. To transpose them from a text where the names were missing or erased to one where they were clear.

An emblem can be a name. Not an obvious or recognizable one, perhaps. Nevertheless, images, as every poet knows, are themselves a nomenclature. They give identity to something. They provide a short title for the mystery.

I found an emblem for her even before I realized I would find it difficult to name her life. Or my own. It happened one Sunday afternoon when I was married with young children. I

32

went to an antiques fair—really just a collection of different stalls—in a hotel in South Dublin.

I remember the afternoon clearly. Or perhaps, like all such memories, it is a composite of other afternoons like that. In any case, the air seems to have been cold and delicate. I do remember looking with surprise, since it was only the third week in February, at the small debris of blossoms on the paths and in the gutters. The hotel was on the coast and looked out on the strand, where in the distance the water was cold, wrinkled metal. Even the gulls looked cold.

I felt the chill and hurried into the hotel. There was a room with long tables and small glass cases. I walked along slowly, staring at lace and frames and cups with cracked rims.

I wish now that I had looked more closely at one item. I remember the dealer pointing and talking. This, she told me, was a lava cameo. An unusual brooch and once fashionable. Unlike the ordinary Victorian cameos, which were carved on shells, this one was cut into volcanic rock. The brooch was a small oval. The face was carved into stone the color of spoiled cream. I looked at it quickly and moved on.

Her name. Her emblem. There was a complexity for me remembering the cameo, and the more I thought about it, the more complex it became. To inscribe a profile in the cold rock. To cut a human face into what had once flowed, fiery and devouring, past farms and villages and livestock. To make a statement of something which was already a statement of random and unsparing destruction. All these acts were very far from being simple. They were ironic and self-conscious.

They employed artifice and irony. They put the stamp of human remembrance on the material of natural destruction.

Such acts of irony and artifice were not congenial to me. I could not remember the brooch in detail. Nevertheless, something about it, in memory, had almost the flavor of an elaborate sarcasm. If I remembered her life, if I were to set her down—a half-turned-away face in its context of ill luck and erased circumstance—would I be guilty of sarcastic craftsmanship? Would I too be making a statement of irony and corruption?

The more I thought of it, the more the lava cameo seemed an emblem of something desperate. If it was a witticism in the face of terror, if it made an ornament of it, what else was memory? Yet in the end, in my need to make a construct of that past, it came down to a simple fact. I had no choice.

2.

I had no choice. That may well be the first, the most enduring characteristic of influence. What's more, I knew nothing. One morning I was woken before dawn, dressed in a pink cardigan and skirt, put in a car, taken to an airport. I was five. My mother was with me. The light of the control tower at Collinstown Airport—it would become Dublin Airport—came through the autumn darkness. I was sick on the plane, suddenly and neatly, into the paper bag provided for the purpose.

I left behind fractions of place and memory, images which would expose slowly. There was a lilac bush I had pulled at so often its musk stayed under my fingernails for days. I would remember the unkempt greenness of the canal where it divided Leeson Street. The lock was made of splintery wood, and boys dived from its narrow platform in summer. Fields, fragrances, an impression of light and informality—that was all. I held my mother's hand, got into another car. I was in another country.

Hardly anything else that happened to me as a child was as important as this: that I left one country and came to another. That an ordinary displacement made an extraordinary distance between the word *place* and the word *mine*.

◆ ◆ ◆

We had come to London. It was 1950. I have a memory of houses and moving vans, of adult voices late at night. Then we were in a tall house, of dun-colored stone, with a flagstaff fitted to a low balcony. In the hall, through doors which were more like wooden gates, there was a kind of chair I had never seen before. It was black leather, and the top was rounded into a sort of hood, edged with brass buttoning. It was called the Watchman's Chair. I was told a man sat in it all night.

Almost everything about this house was different from the one we had left behind. That had been family sized, with a flight of stone steps and a garden edging out into fields. There had been glasshouses and a raggy brown-and-white terrier called Jimmy. There had been lilac and roses along a stone wall. Nothing about it had the closed-in feel of this street. But that had been the house of a life in Ireland, of an Irishman and his wife and five children. And now my father had gone, all at once, it seemed, from being an Irish civil servant to being an ambassador in London. The life had changed. The house had changed.

I knew I was somewhere else. I knew there was something momentous—and for me alone—in the meaning of the big staircase, with its gilded iron fretwork and its polished balustrade; in the formal carpets, with the emblems of the four provinces of Ireland on them: the harp for Leinster, the red hand for Ulster, the dog and shield for the other two. I knew that the meaning was not good. But what was bad and what was good? Bad, it seemed, was dropping soft toys and metal cars down the stairwell. Bad was making noise and tricking with the fire hoses on every floor. Good was being invisible: spending hours in the sparse playroom on the top floor, with a blank television and the balcony which overlooked a dark, closed-in courtyard.

We turned the armchairs on their side there, day after day, and called them horses, and rode them away from this strange house with fog outside the window and a fiction of home in the carpets on the floor.

♦ ♦ ♦

Exile is not simple. There are Irish emigrant songs which make it sound so; they speak of green shores and farewells. By and large, they fit into Valéry's description of Tennyson's *In*

Memoriam: "the broken heart which runs into many editions." Which is not to deny their melody, but it is a marketable one. In most cases those songs were composed in settled and hard-pressed communities of Irishmen and women—most of them in the New World—to reassure them that they still had noble roots as they branched out in a daylight which was often sordid and dispossessed.

I wanted simplicity. I craved it. At school I would learn Thomas Hood's poem: "I remember, I remember / The house where I was born." But as time went on, I didn't. Such memory as I had was constantly being confused and disrupted by gossip and homily, by the brisk and contingent talk of adults. "Stop that. Settle down. Go to sleep now."

The city I came to offered no simplicity either. The rooms to the east of the house looked out on gardens and railings. But the vista was almost always, that first winter anyway, of a yellow fog. If the windows were open, it drifted smokily at the sill. If the doors were open and you went into the street, you entered a muddled and frightening mime. Passersby were gagged in white handkerchiefs. The lights of buses loomed up suddenly. All I knew of the country was this city; all I knew of this city was its fog.

The first winter passed. In the conventional interpretation of exile I should, child as I was, have missed my home and my country. I should have entered the lift and regret of an emigrant ballad and remembered the Dublin hills, say, and the way they look before rain: heathery and too near. Instead I stared out the window at the convent school I attended in

North London. It was March, my first one in England. A
swell of grass, a sort of hummock, ran the length of the window and beyond. It had been planted with crocuses, purple,
white, yellow. I may not have seen them before; I had certainly never seen so many. There and then I appropriated the
English spring.

♦ ♦ ♦

This was not ordinary nature loving. I was not really a
nature lover anyway. I resisted walks in Hyde Park whenever
I could, and I was restless when we went out at school, paired
off in the dreaded "crocodile," to pick up polished chestnuts
or gather acorns. This was different. Not a season but a place.
Not an observant affection but a thwarted possessiveness: a
rare and virulent homesickness.

Even good poets, Thoreau says, do not see "the west-
ward side of the mountain." They propose instead "a tame
and civil side of nature." My concept of the English spring
was as makeshift, as simplified and marketable to my spirit, as
the vision of Ireland in any emigrant song. English crocuses
were always a brilliant mauve or gold. English cows—I had
heard this somewhere—only grazed in meadows full of but-
tercups, flowers so called because they made the milk richer.
The chaffinch was forever on the orchard bough. In the big
woodlands south of London—I was sure of this, though I had
never seen them—were acres of bluebells, harebells, primroses.

If it was a simplification, if it resembled in this the country of emigrant yearning, they had a common source. An emigrant and an exile are not necessarily the same thing. There is at least an illusion of choice about the first condition although, sooner or later, it will share the desolation of the second. But both need a paradigm: The disoriented intelligence seeks out symmetry. I wanted a shape which was flawless. If I had only known it, I wanted a country where I was the sole citizen, where the season was fixed in the first days of April, where there were no arrivals or departures.

The more I imagined that springtime, the more I became, in my imagination, the Victorian child suited to its impossible poise. It was not difficult. If Aristophanes called Euripides, as he is said to have done, a maker of ragamuffin manikins, maybe the remark can do as well for childhood make-believe. Certainly I had plenty of pictures to work from. There were old encyclopedias in the house with just the images I was looking for: English girls with well-managed hair, with lawn pinafores over sprigged dresses, with stockinged legs and buckled shoes. Alice without the looking glass.

Alice. The Looking Glass. An old England, unshadowed by the anger of the oppressed. It would have made better sense had the country I left behind not been engaged in a rapid and passionate restatement of its own identity. Ireland, after so many centuries, was now a republic. A text was being rewritten. Street names. Laws. School curricula. The writing went on and on. My childhood was merely a phrase in it.

II.

My father enters here: a complicated man and, by all accounts, a Jesuitical negotiator. And a Jesuit boy he had been, going to Clongowes, the boarding school south of Dublin, where James Joyce, twenty years earlier, had wept and broken his glasses. My father may have learned there how to make a concept pliable. Later on, in our adult conversations, he would distinguish between Metternich and Talleyrand; between a diplomat who merely sold himself and one who sold his country.

He was a member of what may have been the last generation of European diplomats whose apprenticeship in pessimism was served between two wars. I see them standing on railway platforms, discoursing and wagering in first-class carriages, taking unreliable planes to theaters of crisis. They offered to chaos their skills of rhetoric and compromise and their unending gifts for finding the appropriate dress. Bowler hats, silk top hats, heavy ivory crepe evening scarves seemed to fill the house, marking my father's exits and entrances. He had been in Paris in the thirties. As assistant secretary at Foreign Affairs he had been one of the caretakers of Ireland's neutrality in the Second World War. During the forties he traveled from Dublin to London, arranging trade agreements, searching out the language, the exact form of words which would bridge the damage of centuries with the practicality of a moment.

41

In a sense, he is an anomalous figure against the backdrop of Irish political passion. While argument raged and the injuries of the Irish Civil War healed slowly, he went about his tasks and his travels. Paris. London. Rome. Photographs from the forties show him in a reticent coat of Irish tweed and a brown fedora. His Parisian training is shown only in the way he holds a pair of calf brown gloves, well folded, on the steps of St. Peter's.

In these journeys his accoutrements were talk and a pursuit of realpolitik. The Irish, after the war, were in need of coal and food and employment abroad—especially in England. It was not a time for expensive gestures or republican intransigence.

Observe him in the forties, just after that war, discussing coal with the Ministry of Supply in London. His country needs it, and he will get it. But the ironies are plentiful. Here is a man who studied classics at Trinity and political science at Harvard. He can quote Thucydides on the costliness of civil strife and Tacitus on the infirmity of rulers. He has a strong sense of historical absurdity and a true sense of patriotism. He will put all and any of that behind the attempt to bring heat and shelter from that country to his own. He will search hard for the right formula of words to achieve it. And yet will anything he says, anything he proposes, have the raw force of the nineteenth-century Fenian cry "Burn everything English but their coal?"

♦ ♦ ♦

There were shadows. His grandfather had been the master of the workhouse in Clonmel. The historical ambiguity of
a forebear who had harnessed his pony and culled his kitchen
garden in the environs of fever and hunger would not have
been lost on him. After all, he served political masters for
whom the fever and hunger of the nineteenth century were
some of the most persistent badges of honor.

His mother—another shadow—was illegitimate. Mar-
ried to his father, a respectable and feared civil servant in the
British service, she had suffered much. Once or twice, at a
later stage, he hinted obliquely at her sufferings: She had kept
to the house a great deal; her closest friend was the house-
keeper.

And there had been—there always was in Ireland—an
eviction. It had happened to the family his mother lived with;
she had been a child at the time. They had been evicted from
a smallholding near the river Barrow in Kildare. There were
almost no details. Just the elegant un-Irish name of Ver-
schoyle was carefully remembered: the hated middleman. But
if there were no details, the image of an eviction was a brutal
Irish generic. No cartoon, no sentimental drawing can have
anything like the force or bitterness of folk memory: the
dreaded bailiff, the furniture out of doors, the windows
barred. The illegitimate child, dispossessed even of a foster
shelter, was enigmatically factored into my father's intelligence. Years later he told me of a childhood memory: of
standing on Dame Street in Dublin, holding his mother's
hand. The viceregal carriage—this may have been in 1910—

clattered out of the gates of Dublin Castle. He went to doff his cap, not an unusual gesture on those streets at that time. His mother pulled away her hand. "Don't do that," she whispered.

Now it was 1948, and Ireland, having been a member of the Commonwealth since 1921, was suddenly, almost improvisationally, declared a republic. There was surprise, even shock. But there were pieces to be picked up, loose ends to be tied. The old profession of diplomacy had everything to do with loose ends and scattered pieces, and so my father was in London. It was the Commonwealth conference, and he was speaking to old colleagues as well as an old oppressor. But his speech had an unusual ending. He wished Canada and Australia well—they had decided to remain in the Commonwealth—and he understood that decision; indeed, he respected it. But the Irish would withdraw. "There is not," he said—and I am going on hearsay and his own account in this—"a cottage in Ireland which has not shuddered at the words 'Open in the name of the king.'"

It was negotiating rhetoric; it was appropriate language. He was a trained man and would not have used it had it not fitted both requirements. But there was also, I am sure of it, an invisible darkness in the language: the parish lands of Kilberry to the east of Athy. In any case, Ireland was now a republic and needed an ambassador. And he was it.

I knew nothing. Nothing of nations or that Napoleon said, "What is history but a fable agreed upon?" The truth was that by such words, such gestures—by hints and transits, negotiations and compromises I was utterly oblivious of—my fate was decided together with my country's. By a strange, compound irony, the same sequence of events which made me a citizen of a republic had determined my exile from it.

When night came, I balanced a heavy maroon volume on the sheet—the books had been carefully covered for me by my mother—and I was out in the air of an English spring. Never mind that I was called Ginger and Carrot-Top at school, that I had freckles and an accent. I was wearing muslin and those shoes, or maybe boots with impossible mother-of-pearl buttons joining the silky leather from toe to shin, which needed the curve of a silver buttonhook to undo. I was looking for a thrush's nest. I was in those places for which the English had fragrant, unfamiliar names: a copse; an orchard; a meadow. In the Irish usage they would have been mere fields and gardens. I was picking bluebells and primroses, going home with indigo- and lemon-colored handfuls. I was going home to muffins and clear, swirling tea surrounded by flowered porcelain. Then it was time for the light to be switched off, for the room to fill with shadows and lamplight.

"Language is fossil poetry," says Emerson, and it may well be. But it is also home truth. Whatever the inventions and distortions of my imaginings, my tongue, the sounds it made in my mouth, betrayed me. I was no English Alice. I was an Irish child in England. The more time went on, the more my confusion grew. I knew, if only by vague apprehensions, what I did not own; I had no knowledge of what I did. The other children at school had a king and a country. They could be casual about the bluebells and chaffinches. They could say "orchard" instead of "garden" with the offhand grace imparted by nine-tenths of the law. I could not. When the king died and the reverend mother announced the fact to the whole school at lunchtime, the other children knew how to weep. I only knew how to admire their tears.

The inevitable happened. One day my tongue betrayed me out of dream and counterfeit into cold truth. I was in the cloakroom at school in the middle of the afternoon. A winter darkness was already gathering through one of the stubborn fogs of the time. A teacher was marshaling children here and there, dividing those who were taking buses from those who were being collected. "I amn't taking the bus," I said. I was six or seven then, still within earshot of another way of speaking. But the English do not use that particular construction. It is an older usage. If they contract the verb and the negative, they say, "I'm not."

Without knowing, I had used that thing for which the English reserve a visceral dislike: their language, loaded and aimed by the old enemy. The teacher whirled around. She corrected my grammar; her face set, her tone cold. "You're not in Ireland now" was what she said.

♦ ♦ ♦

Exile, like memory, may be a place of hope and delusion. But there are rules of light there and principles of darkness, something like a tunnel, in fact. The further you go in, the less you see, the more you know your location by a brute

absence of destination. Later I read this definition in a nineteenth-century book for children: "Home—the nursery of
the infinite."

The trouble was, I was adrift in a place of finite detail. I
could have been a character who had woken from a lyric
fever in an old novel, unable to remember a name, a place of
origin or the faces of those who had kept vigil. And there the
chapter ends and a new one begins. A cup of tea is brought; a
miniature oil painting; a sweet-smelling elbow-length glove.
The character begins to remember: in glamorous fractions, in
lightning flashes of recall.

One day in the playroom, with the television off as
usual, but the chairs upright and returned to their nonequine
positions, I found a book. It was thick and well bound. The
illustrations were drawings of landscape and figures, with stories as well as legends. I was not a particularly enthusiastic
reader. My best adventures in comprehension, and all my ef-
forts of attention, were reserved for the maroon encyclopedia
at the end of the day. But I was older now, maybe only a year
or two, but enough to make me look at things more skepti-
cally, more curiously.

The pages were not glossy. They were mat and pastel,
and the pictures were reprints of watercolors. Here was a blue
distance; there was a bog with the flat ditch brown squares
neatly cut. At the side of a ditch were clumps of scutch grass
and smudges of ivory and green on stilts: the artist's rendering
of cow parsley. On the far side were red fuchsias, the flowers
of the west of Ireland, veterans of salt air and limestone soil. I

could see that it was summer. A cart was drawn up by the roadside with a donkey in the traces. His big ears—they were the black-brown of cocoa, I thought—were up and forward.

I turned the page. This was the story of someone called Michael. This bog, this donkey, these distances were part of his home. But he was leaving home. He was going away from this place with its weedy cow parsley, its shadows of fuchsia. "I am leaving here," he said in the text, "because Ireland has nothing to offer me but a spade."

I turned the page again. Now there was no donkey, no cold brown distance. Instead there was a woman sitting on a throne, holding a harp. She wore loose clothes, draped in folds, and one shoulder was bare. "Hibernia," it said under the picture. And the line "O harp of my country." I put the book down. I was confused and startled. Was this the place I had heard of? Was this what it offered? This strange mix of music and a wooden-handled implement I had hardly ever seen? I thought about it. No one I knew used one. We had no garden.

♦ ♦ ♦

My father was a good pianist. At Harvard in the twenties he had made spare cash as the pianist in a jazz band. At the University of Chicago he continued his studies in political science and his piano playing: thumping out ragtime and Dixie, turning up on winter afternoons in a vicuña coat. One afternoon in rehearsal—the band was preparing for a college dance—the saxophonist stopped playing. He looked at my father. "You play a mean piano," he said. And resumed.

He no longer played jazz. He had to climb up three flights of stairs to get to the piano. It stood against one wall of the playroom, opposite the window, its polished black covers almost always closed. When he opened them, it was not to play songs like "Toot Toot Tootsie"—*if you don't get a letter then you'll know I'm in jail*—although he still whistled them at times. Almost always he came up in the late afternoon, his Sweet Afton cigarette glowing between his fingers, then between his lips as he lifted the cover. Almost always he played the songs of Tom Moore.

♦ ♦ ♦

Poor Tom Moore. I have come to think of him that way. Tom Moore, who, according to Byron, "struck his wild lyre while listening dames were hushed." He was born the son of a Dublin grocer, and he had studied law at Trinity, as did my father. He was the friend of Robert Emmet, who lost his life in the aftermath of the '98 rebellion. And who, when I was a teenager, would seem the exemplary Irish hero.

A year later Moore had crossed the Irish Channel, from Dublin to London. He was twenty-one. It was a good time to go and a better one to leave. Ahead of him were the Middle Temple and literary celebrity. Behind him Ireland was in flames. From Dublin to Galway, from Kildare to Wexford, the repercussions of the 1798 rebellion were still being felt.

The gibbets remained against the skyline. The terrible stories of pitch-and-tar cappings were still traveling from village to village in Wexford. The heroes of the rebellion, Emmet, Tone, Fitzgerald, were either dead or about to be. And their ideas—what Yeats called "All that delirium of the brave"—were over for a generation.

Poor Tom Moore. In British drawing rooms, with his sweet tenor voice, singing his own Irish melodies, he brought tears to the eyes of his listeners. Most of them were ladies; many of them were the wives of the landlords and militia who were even then, at that very moment, against the backdrop of his songs, looting and burning and murdering and evicting.

My father climbed the stairs. He opened the piano. He began to play. With flat-spread, nicotine-stained fingers. He played "Oft in the Stilly Night" and "Believe Me If All Those Endearing Young Charms" and "The Minstrel Boy."

And why not? A century and a half before he had come to London as a diplomat representing Ireland, these songs had preceded him in the role. They had sweet-talked and compromised their way into British drawing rooms, guaranteeing that the Irish question would be a matter of cadence and the English response a modicum of sentiment.

The tune lilted up and down. I closed my eyes, opened them, closed them again. I looked away from the smoke. And stood there on the top floor of a building on a fogbound English afternoon—a building that was itself a fiction of nationhood—listening to other fictions.

The expatriate is in search of a country; the exile in

search of a self. He or she learns how to look for it in a territory between rhetoric and reality, with its own customs and habits of mind, its preferred speech and rigorous invention. I may have heard the song so many times I was bored by it. I may have felt the malaise and displacement of that upper room, stranded in a city of nowheres. But I was learning something. Tom Moore was a survivor. In a time of transition and danger, he had understood that safety is not a place but a language. In his search for a nation, he had discovered that above all.

3.

IN SEARCH OF A NATION

T here was a time in my life when I searched for a nation. Beyond friendship, beyond social ease, it was what I wanted to find. I was fifteen and sixteen—a time of unreason and instinct. And it was not a reasonable quest in any case. If I return to it now, it is in an attempt to find a private history within the public one.

♦ ♦ ♦

I am reading a book. It is a cold March afternoon in
New York. I have lived in the city for three years since my
family moved here from London. I have grown to love the
place, with its finned cars and theatrical weather. The carousel
in Central Park. The metal-colored freeze-up of the lake.
The bricks too hot to walk on in summer. I eat hot dogs and
listen to Buddy Holly. I show signs of becoming an American
teenager.

But now at fourteen, suddenly, I have grown restless. I
have started, in a scattered and disordered way, reading Irish
poems and stories. Today it is a poem by Padraic Pearse,
found in a book on my mother's shelf. The note at the back
tells me—I do not remember knowing it—that he was exe-
cuted in 1916 for his part in capturing the General Post Office
in Dublin at the time of the Easter Rebellion. The poem is
called "The Fool." It is a big, spread-out biblical piece, with a
wide rhetoric and a harsh tone. But I see nothing of this.
What I see is the way a poem about nationhood has suddenly
included me, as other poems I have read recently, about
memory or landscape, do not. The inclusion is not by address
or invocation but by a sweeping and self-proposing act of
language that speaks to all the longings I have for grandilo-
quence and certainty:

*I have squandered the splendid years that the Lord God
gave to my youth
In attempting impossible things,*

53

deeming them alone worth the toil.
Was it folly or grace? Not men shall judge me, but God.
I have squandered the splendid years:
Lord if I had the years I would squander them over again.

I put the book down and walk to the window. Sixteen
stories down, the East River flows towards the city. The
freighters and barges make their way across a surface where
light is broken up into patches and squares of dazzle. I can see
Queens in the distance. Long Island is somewhere out there as
well. Other water. Other land. But somewhere far away was
a place a man had died for. Made of rivers and cities. Where
water was struck by light in just this way. Which had the same
name as my country. Which was my country.

◆ ◆ ◆

It is a few months later. My parents are entertaining visitors. My mother points out an elderly man. He is talking to
someone else at a sideways angle. He has a high color and a
sweet mouth, and he is, my mother tells me, a poet. His name
is Padraic Colum. I recognize it from the same anthology of
Irish poetry in which I read the Pearse poem. What I have no
way of knowing is his own difficult history as an Irish poet,
which one day will seem to me a proof of the exclusions and
infirmities of a tradition we will come to share. I know nothing about his birth in the Midlands or his first book of poems.
Or Yeats's co-option of him as a suitable rural poet for the

Irish Revival. Or, indeed, his disillusion and exile from Ireland, which are the reason he stands here talking to someone as an American dark gathers outside the window.

At the end of the evening I follow him to the elevator. He has put on a coat and a felt hat with a small brim, which tilts forward and to the side. I start to say something. He turns towards me. "Did you," I ask suddenly, "know Padraic Pearse?" He looks at me for a moment. "Yes, I did," he says.

It is the answer I want. In the broken world of my childhood a sparkling continuum is established. Between action and language. Between poet and patriot.

II.

I came back to Ireland when I was fourteen. I saw unfamiliar sights: horses and lamplight and the muddy curve of the Liffey. I grew to know street names and bus timetables. I went to live with my sisters in a flat outside the city. I went to boarding school. I studied for exams. I started to explore the word *Irish,* not this time as a distant fact but as the close-up reality of my surroundings. As a word which painted letter boxes and colored trains. Which framed laws and structured language.

Language. At first this was what I lacked. Not just the historic speech of the country. I lacked that too, but so did others. This was a deeper loss; I returned to find that my vocabulary of belonging was missing. The street names, the meeting places—it was not just that I did not know them. It was something more. I had never known them. I had lost not only a place but the past that goes with it and, with it, the clues from which to construct a present self.

I had to learn a new sensory idiom. A fog in the mouth, for example, which was different from the London one: less gritty, with more of an ocean aftertaste. An unkempt greenness on the streets. A drizzle which was interseasonal, constant. Different trees. Different birds.

As I learned these things, the last unwanted gift of exile came to me. I began to watch places with an interest so exact it might have been memory. There was that street corner, with the small newsagent which sold copies of the *Irish Independent* and honeycomb toffee in summer. I could imagine myself there, a child of nine, buying peppermints and walking back down by the canal, the lock brown and splintered as ever, and boys diving from it.

It became a powerful impulse, a slow and intense reconstruction of a childhood which had never happened. A fragrance or a trick of light was enough. Or a house I entered which I wanted not just to appreciate but to remember, and then I would begin. Here was the hall with its parquet flower, the sideboard with white lilac and a gilded mirror. There were the photographs of the children and the kennel outside for the dog. I had been eleven here, playing with a friend in that garden. I had been six. I could remember the croquet game in summer, the skirts of women, the intent frowns of the players.

There was a small seaside town outside Drogheda called

Clogher Head. I had missed it by a small action, by a form of words. Now I thought myself back into it: summer days when the rain cleared and the roads were vacant. A bicycle lying sideways on the main street, and a brown and white dog barking. Red lemonade sold in long bottles. And the vista full of bathers and fishing boats, and the grit of sand as it came out of shoes and towels. And I, in a room where light came through the curtains until an hour before midnight, lying down to sleep. An Irish child.

III.

Irish. If I could not remember a country, I could at least imagine a nation. I was not searching for a dialogue; I was looking to disappear into powerful images: the narrow back ways of a British town where a shot was fired, a man was captured and the refrain of a ballad was made inevitable. A channel of water where French sailing ships creaked and heaved. A gibbet, its outline visible for miles against a Wexford horizon.

Imagination. The word itself has the poignance of opposites. By imagining a nation, I was beginning the very process, awakening the very faculty which would bring me into conflict with it. I was building a strength which would discover a weakness in these images. But at the time those oppositions seemed unlikely. I had returned home. The country was changing. Nevertheless, the exterior reality still supported something very like patriotism. There were festivals and remembrances. Newspapers referred easily and often to the past. The city was marked with buildings, corners, alleyways where a hero had died; a point had been proved.

I listened out for the references. I looked intently at the buildings. I read book after book and remembered names and actions. But I knew in my heart, I never forgot it, that I was not the same as other Irish children. Like a daughter in a legend, I had been somewhere else. I had eaten different foods. I had broken the spell of place and family. By that logic alone I could not return.

IV.

The issue between an artist and a nation is not a faith but a self. The creative self must be complex and earned; the national self is ardent and singular, bent to the collective and determined to serve it.

At sixteen, once I had returned to Ireland, my life was both obedient and disordered. I stayed here and went there. I lived in a flat when I was not at boarding school. I was reading poetry and trying to write it. But when I took a piece of paper and began to write those first poems, even through the borrowed images and false gestures, I saw the existence and demand of a preliminary self. I had no language for it, and no wish for it. The vague sense of a future, where sexuality and memory, childhood and language would have to meet, was more a threat than a hope. The images of the nation were moving and compelling for that reason: They gathered the will into action; they turned the action into heroism.

I was beginning to see the power of landscape, mostly,

however, as cityscape. The relation of stone to water, and the way granite after dark or rain gave off a sort of streetlight, and the vivid streets and neighborhoods of Dublin, all drew me in.

On Sunday afternoons, with time off school, or on Easter holidays, I would take a series of buses into the middle of the city. First from Killiney village, through Dun Laoghaire and along the coast for a while, with its strand and chimneys, leaning and turning to see the pinpoints of cantering ponies. Another bus into Stephen's Green. Then I was free to walk around, looking at streets and back lanes. I had no coherent idea of where the town ended and the country began, of how the past inscribed itself in this place or that. I had no local history.

Even so I began to realize—although some of this must be the work of hindsight—how hard it was to extricate place from nation. The names, the memories, even the inches of ground had become proof of pride and sacrifice. But these are not the thoughts or the words of a teenager. If I take an example now, I am arguing as a woman and not the girl who stood outside St. Catherine's Church in Thomas Street one September afternoon. Who was told that Robert Emmet had been hanged here, in that month, in 1803.

♦ ♦ ♦

Emmet. September. The hero and the month of my birth. The beautiful opening act of winter when corners of Stephen's Green at dusk looked like a smoking room after midnight: a bluish haze, convivial and promising. The smell of leaves burning in crisp piles. The mulberry leaves drying out and the rowanberries turning scarlet. And a man hanged by the neck until he died.

He was hanged on a September day. The executioner asked twice, three times on the scaffold, "Are you ready, sir?" Then—after Emmet replied, "Not yet"—lost patience and opened the trapdoor. After half an hour his body was cut down, his head cut off, and the hangman walked the wooden platform, holding it and saying, "This is the head of Robert Emmet." Hard to believe that despite his end, he had been a real man. A young man. Hardly more than a boy in the winter of 1802, as he moved around Dublin, talking at dinner tables, over the salt cellars and crystal of a doomed and temporary Protestant nation, keeping his counsel. A flesh-and-blood man in the city where he would die.

◆ ◆ ◆

And this is where, outside St. Catherine's Church, before my eyes and the eyes of that teenager, Robert Emmet disappears. He vanishes into soft words, garbled accounts of his speech from the dock. He becomes legend and excuse. He drifts, in a slow haze of half-truths, into memories that are neither clear nor accurate. He becomes romantic fable and nationalist invention. And in so doing, he describes the typical trajectory of the nationalist hero: from action to image. From event to invention.

In Emmet's case it was almost immediate. Within a few years of his death, his friend Tom Moore has turned him into a soft option. "O breathe not his name, let it sleep in the shade," he writes of him. The song was to be sung to the air of "The Red Fox." Moore reminisced happily about the sources of its inspiration: "How little did I then think in one of the most touching of the sweet airs I used to play to him, his own dying words would find an interpreter so worthy of their sad but proud feeling."

In the fastness of British drawing rooms, in the safe company of aristocrats and liberals, Moore knew exactly how much Irish patriotism was acceptable, and how little. Emmet became a fiction. Into that fiction were subsumed all the awkwardness, all the untidy events of conspiracy. Into it went the strained features of the young man who kept his hopes and seditions hidden in the winter of 1802. Into it went a hope for freedom. Out of it came the words of pre-Victorian sentiment—a strategy as effective in making rebellion safe as any spy or warrant from Dublin Castle.

◆ ◆ ◆

And so the continuum between poet and patriot, between language and action was not what I had thought. It was not a solid and useful bridge across which a history moved to safety. Instead it was a soft and flawed connection, where words undid actions and actions could never be free of their consequences in language. For every death there would be a ballad. In every ballad the brokenhearted transactions between drawing room and street corner, and between English liberal and Irish rebel, would be stated and restated.

It is hard enough at fifteen and sixteen to know anything, and I knew less than most. I had lost the free speech of childhood. I was overintense and ready to seize on the wrong details. I found it hard to make my way from season to season, taking for granted the signposts that led to adulthood. My years away had given me a crooked respect for episodes. And here was a history rich in them. Here was an admixture of folly and locale and love of place. And it was hard to resist. Above all, it was hard to deny the force of this particular episode.

Outside a church on the north side of a city a scaffold had been built. Windows had shut and doors closed to the sound of that hammering. Autumn light had fallen on raw wood. A man had died there. I knew in my mind, in my intellect, through my reading of poetry, that place could be free of taint. Could be an imaginative design where freedom from exile and estrangement was found. And yet it was hard to look at the streets with their cowled streetlamps, to look at the hills at the end of them and to disentangle the idea of those stones and blues from the idea of a man who died. For this. And this. And this.

v.

In my own way I understood the pageantry and tension behind the idea of a nation. The gibbets. The coffin ships. I saw it through the glass of exile, by which the glamour of ownership was greatly magnified. But I was too young to understand that part of a nation which would come to chal-

lenge and exclude me as a woman and an artist: its sexual
drama.

The teenage years, for any young person, have enough
sexual drama. I was growing up, away from my parents, moving towards language and desire at the same time, but not at
the same speed. I was awkward and dreamy. I looked in mirrors. I thought of a future with love and pleasure in it, but
without location.

In the midst of those uncertainties, the nation, at least for
a time, was a definite and sharp reality. It happened. It gathered. It was an irreducible part of an everyday life. I looked at
the shamrocks, the wolfhounds, even the crude likenesses of
the 1916 patriots with uncritical eyes. I listened to and used
the dialect of patriotism. *Martyr. Sacrifice. Our own.* And if
there was a hidden drama, to some extent it was concealed by
the sheer eloquence of the cause and my own need for that
eloquence. Viewed from a distance, the story of the nation
was a narrative of destiny. A small island, next to a larger one,
loses both territory and language. And, after centuries of oppression, recovers part of one and less of the other. Not a
fortunate story, but a compelling one.

♦ ♦ ♦

I need to pause here. I need to remember that at sixteen
and seventeen I loved that narrative. A back street. The slime
of cobbles near the river. A single shot undoing a century of
humiliation. Or so it seemed. The individual act of courage
drew me in. I carried the melody of patriotism with me as I

came into the ordinary daylight of the city, as I passed Coca-Cola signs and advertisements for caricatures. I took books down from the shelves in libraries and the houses of friends. I read with wonder and enthusiasm.

I had, to accompany my discoveries, a powerful literature of protest and remembrance. Coming to my seventeenth birthday, I was reading the *Jail Journal* of John Mitchel. There in a black, staccato prose were the hinge and swing of the whole legend. Born in Derry, Mitchel had gone to Trinity College, as I would. He had founded the *Nation* newspaper with other patriots in 1842. In May of 1848, after the collapse of an ill-conceived rebellion, he was tried for sedition, found guilty and sentenced to fourteen years' transportation. And so here he was, in a beautiful early-summer twilight, steaming out of Dublin Bay on a prison ship. "Dublin city with its bay and pleasant villas," he wrote, "city of bellowing slaves, villas of genteel dastards—lies now behind us, and the sun has set behind the blue peaks of Wicklow, as we steam past Bray Head, where the vale of Shanganagh, sloping softly from the Golden spears, sends its bright river murmuring to the sea. And I am on the first stage of my way, faring to what regions of unknown horror? And may never never—never more, O, Ireland—my mother and queen!—see vale or hill or murmuring stream of thine."

A dark violence blurred by Victorian sentiment. At first it was an irresistible mix. I read in starts and stops through the nineteenth century. The poems, speeches, ballads. Only gradually, and then only with a half awareness, did the sexual

drama begin to unfold. Only in fractions and pieces of information and reflection did I begin to notice certain things: that
the clairvoyance I needed to enter that theater of action and
danger demanded a troubling androgyny. If I wanted to be in
those back streets, to speak in those conspiracies, I would
have to be male. The male, after all, was an active principle,
inviting admiration. And I was a teenage girl, looking not just
to admire but to belong. Yet how could I belong to these
actions, dreamed up by men and carried out by them? The
fact is that teenage dreams of action and heroism are filled
with exciting and impossible transpositions of sexuality. In
those dreams I would wear the green tailcoat or crop my head
or carry a revolver. If I wanted to feel the power of nation as
well as its defeat, then I would take on the properties of the
hero. I would raid a barracks for arms or write a note the night
before my execution under the bluish sputter of a gas flame. I
would crack my head against a pavement north of the Liffey
as I fell, wounded to death by British bullets. And as soon as
my head—a male, thick-necked head—touched the stone, I
would dissolve into refrains and stanzas. I would pass from
hero to apotheosis.

But I was uneasy. Gradually, in inches, not yards, I began
to realize that this idea of a nation, for all its lore and invention, had ugly limits. For those empathies, those androgynies
to exist, I had to make myself available for reconstruction. I
could not, for a start, be quick or skeptical. I could not even
be the untidy teenager that I was, moving between houses
and schools and flats, looking for a home and unready to find

65

one. I had to be prepared, with each encounter, to open my heart and close my mind.

And yet if you took the hero out of the story, what was left? What female figure was there to identify with? There were no women in those back streets. None, at least, who were not lowly auxiliaries of the action. The heroine, as such, was utterly passive. She was Ireland or Hibernia. She was stamped, as a rubbed-away mark, on silver or gold; a compromised regal figure on a throne. Or she was a nineteenth-century image of girlhood, on a frontispiece or in a book of engravings. She was invoked, addressed, remembered, loved, regretted. And, most important, died for. She was a mother or a virgin. Her hair was swept or tied back, like the prow of a ship. Her flesh was wood or ink or marble. And she had no speaking part. If her harvests were spoiled, her mother tongue wiped out, her children killed, then it was for someone else to mark the reality. Her identity was as an image. Or was it a fiction?

Caught between these realities, I grew more and more unsettled. I had no exact words for how I felt. But after a while I was less free in my adventures. Gradually my re-creation of the back streets, my sense of the glamour of a single action were being undermined. I was having to see the story within the story. I was starting to notice the absence of my name in it. I was feeling the sexual opposites within the narrative. The intense passivity of the female; the fact that to the male principle was reserved the right not simply of action but of expression as well. I was ready to weep or sing or recite in the cause of Ireland. To do any of that, however, I would have to change from the young girl who looked with increasing interest at the faces and shapes of boys. I would have to give up the body and spirit of a woman. If I chose to keep them, then my tears would dry out, my mouth would close, my words would disappear. I was restive and disappointed at the choices offered to me. And, in a certain sense, unclear. And there was something else: If the passive images of Ireland—the queen, the silver stamp—were so present in songs and remembrances, what had happened to the others? To the women who had survived. And those who had not.

VI.

In a summer dusk, when I was seventeen, my mother told me a story. I was leaning across a chair, facing a window. Back out towards the river, which ran behind the house, the sky was still bright; everything else was darkening. The fruit trees were spare and dark—a child's drawing. The apples were black globes.

The story she told was about her mother. She had been born into a family of millers and had been one of thirteen children. She had married very young, a seaman who became a sea captain. She had died after the birth of her last child—my mother—at thirty-one in a Dublin hospital.

It was a short conversation. My mother spoke only rarely about the past. It was, in its way, a small piece of an oral tradition, told in a summer dusk and in a halting way. Of a woman she could not remember. Who had been deserted by good luck and had left five orphan daughters. There was nothing heroic in her account, and she offered no meanings. Instead she did what innumerable human beings have done with their children: She told me what had happened.

VII.

My grandmother lived outside history. And she died there. A thirty-one-year-old woman, with five daughters, facing death in a hospital far from her home—I doubt that anything around her mattered then. Yet in her lifetime Ireland had gone from oppression to upheaval. A language had been reclaimed. Laws had changed. Conspiracies and explosions were everyday occurrences. And she had existed at the edge of it.

Did she find her nation? And does it matter? In one sense it does. Throughout the decade and a half in which she bore her children and moved nearer to her death, her country was restating itself in forceful and painful ways. Take 1887, for instance. During the spring of that year twenty-five Fenians were sentenced to long terms of penal servitude. Among them was Tom Clarke, who would endure English prison and emerge to die, before a British firing squad. In the same year the Congress of the Gaelic Athletic Association met in Thurles.

It was a stormy meeting. When a priest in Nenagh tried to propose a different candidate for chairman of the meeting from the local Fenian, there was an immediate split between the clerical and Fenian members of the association. Imagine the scene. The tables bare and pushed aside. The flushed faces and scattered papers. The moon hanging outside, over a town, over a field. The man who raises a fist in the doorway and shouts about another man's betrayal.

Small events. Local frictions. And yet I wonder whether she turned in some corridor, looked up from some moment of play and heard the whispers and gossip which, by their force, suggested a wider truth. Did she hear in some muttered conversation the future of an armed struggle, the music of anger, the willingness to die? I doubt it. If she looked up at all, I believe that she was listening for her life—for some intonation in a voice which told her of simple love or downright annoyance.

And what was I listening for? Three-quarters of a century on, I lifted my head, I looked up. What troubled me, increasingly, was not whether she had included the nation in her short life. But whether that nation had included her.

VIII.

What is this thing—a nation—that is so powerful it can make songs, attract sacrifice and so exclusive it drives into hiding the complex and skeptical ideas which would serve it best?

I would come to wonder in later years how a nation is made, how it continues to be made. Whether the whispers of an assassination, gathering force in back rooms and safe houses, guarantee it. Whether the ballad hummed after midnight in an empty street assists it. Whether its real energy lies in conspiracy or celebration. As I walked the streets, looking at green buses and letter boxes, at street names marked in Irish, I could see the visible signs of it. Its invisible life I was less sure of.

And here was the clue. The making of a nation—I would come to see this—lies not in codes or names but in its power to construct its unseen inner life from the minds and memories of those who live in it. To turn inhabitants into citizens and citizens into patriots.

For a season I was both. I have to look back and see a girl finding her way slowly in the outer world of a city yet relatively swiftly in the inner world which was its inference. My intelligence was a jumble of refrains and battles. I knew the names of men caught into obscure treasons; I knew the addresses of prisons in odd parts of the British Isles. I belonged to myself and to my country insofar as I could translate that self into that country. If I had continued in that moment, then the invisible nation would have continued its progress. An architecture of songs, roads, ambush sites and old graveyards would have built slowly. It would have taken over my ability to see landscape and my judgment of the last chapter of a book.

But it did not happen. I was reading other books. I was hearing other reminiscences. There were other lives—the lives, for instance, given over to language rather than action—which seemed to me exemplary. I was building within myself the hope that I also could live that life of language. I was starting to feel—although this may make it more conscious than it was—that the silent feminine imagery in the lore of the nation went badly with my active determination to be a poet.

It is not so hard to make a picture of one person's search for a nation. It is, after all, a subjective business. It is much harder to draw the map of the imaginative faculty which is threatened by that search. I wanted to find and belong to my country's powerful version of history. I found that the imagination I was beginning to sense in myself—perhaps only in a rudimentary feeling for language—was limited and constrained by that version. To understand the difficult oppositions between that version and the life of the imagination, I would have to go further and look harder. It would be lonely work.

4.

IN SEARCH OF A LANGUAGE

I worked, almost alone, in a study above gardens that looked out to sea. It was my final year at school. In the distance were Bray Head and the Sugarloaf Mountain. Nearby were the palms and steep declines of the Vico Road. Behind me as I studied was a copse of evergreens which sheltered the school from the road. If you turned over your shoulder and looked at the treetops, it was just possible to see the water flash and spoil their darkness.

My solitude was circumstantial. I had returned to Ireland in my teens; I had no knowledge of the Irish language. Therefore, I had to do the General Certificate of the British system. I was an erratic, hit-and-miss student, averse to discipline and hardly able to connect my intense reading of poetry with any other part of my studies.

The study where I worked was a somber room, with a scarred oval table and two armchairs. There were embroideries on the armrests, a bookshelf with just a few paperbacks leaning crookedly against one another. And a bay window. A wireless with a dial and a coarsely woven front grid stood on a lamp table in the corner. Under the window was a eucalyptus tree, a glittering exhibition which distracted me when the sea winds came in with the spring light behind them.

I see myself there, more than I do in other places. My first retrospective glance shows me one of the important rooms of my life. One quick look is enough to take in the wide half curve of its shape—the bay in the distance, the eucalyptus leaves and myself bent over a single book.

I was learning Latin. I had been learning it for years, since I was eleven or twelve, but only in the formal and resistant way of most students at that time. But in the previous year it had become obvious that I would do it for my final exams, if only by default. I was not glad to do it. It was a harsh and complicated subject. The texts were extensive. The corn-colored oblong of *Arnold's Grammar* was a bleak prospect. But I had no choice. And so, since the previous year, I had been coming up to the study over the bay and, without any other company, engaging with a language I did not love, under the eye of a teacher who hardly thought me fit to learn it.

My Latin teacher was a small woman, narrow-shouldered and with a rocking walk, who smoked heavily and was exasperated at the sight of me—at least at first. By her lights, I was one of these students thrust upon her and the Latin language by a circumstance of education. She was irascible and forthright; any mistake immediately corresponded with a sound in her throat, halfway between a word and a guttural of anger. She almost always wore a scarf around her neck, tied in a jaunty way below her collar. When it began to move forwards and backwards, I would know, with my head bent to the page, that her head was turning in exasperation. I would see the nicotine stain on her index finger as she moved it on the lines and listen for the fury to begin in her throat.

Throughout my sixteenth year we struggled with grammar. I hated it. She detested my lack of preparation, my panicky guesswork and my wandering attention. I sat with my back to the window—to the sea, the glossy leaves of the eucalyptus, the whole theatrical array of lights and shadow which a coastal scene provides. To the right and left of my chair were tall side windows. I could look sideways and see a thrush in the frost, beating a snail on a stone. I could watch friends walking to and from class, carrying tennis rackets and hockey sticks, laughing and talking, free of the burdens and worries of a dead grammar. I envied them.

Then one day in my last year—although this is a figurative use of time—I began to understand something. It was something about the economy of it all: the way the ablative absolute gathered and compressed time. One day, again figuratively, it was a burdensome piece of grammar. The next, with hardly any warning, it was a messenger with quick heels and a bright face. I hardly knew what had happened. I began to respect, however grudgingly, the systems of a language which could make such constructs that, although I had no such words for it, they stood against the disorders of love or history. They had described bridges and defined governments. They had left the mouth of the centurion and entered the mind of a Sicilian farm worker. They had forged alliances and named stars. And at that point of my adolescence, where the words I wrote on a page were nothing but inexact, the precision and force of these constructs began to seem both moving and and healing.

At last the teacher and I began to have something in common. I looked less out of the side window, down at the other pupils, with their more leisurely schedules, their command of another language, their sense of home. The bay changed, from a postcard scene to a backdrop for adventure. I no longer guessed so wildly. I began to see how syntax can discover purpose. I studied only one other subject—English —and the hours I spent studying Latin began to command most of my attention.

It was not rapid; it was gradual. But gradually the constructs I had hated, the long hours spent at dusk trying to prepare for the following day's lesson began to give way to a sense of power. I had never known words as power. They had

75

been the fragments and ambiguities of place. The quick commands of a rushed kitchen: "Sit down. Put that away. Don't
touch that." Or else they had been words to cover the wound
and insult of the place which was not your own: *London. The
king. Land of Hope and Glory.* Now they were a sinuous path
to clarity and safety.

Sometimes I returned to the study in the evening, when
the bay and the hills had almost disappeared, and the gardens
were going dark, intending to work on a Latin passage. The
eucalyptus tree was a black shape. Maybe a fishing trawler on
its way back to the pier at Dun Laoghaire would be a tiny
lacework of lights. And there I still am: a girl bent over a
book, draped by dusk and ocean light, in a country where no
Roman occupation ever happened, where no walls were built
and no infrastructure made. I am there, learning the syntax
which stops time and commands logic. Behind me are a sea
which those words never navigated and a distance which they
never measured.

♦ ♦ ♦

There is a defining moment which comes early in a
poet's life. A moment full of danger. It happens at the very
edge of becoming a poet, when behind there is nothing but
the mute terrain where, until then, a life has been lived and
felt without finding its formalization.

In my case that mute backward-reaching distance was
my own childhood. It had been lived out of my country,
away from the signals and clues by which a self, almost without knowing it, finds its way to adulthood. The moment of

danger for me, as for other poets, came when it looked at last that silence would yield to expression. At that split second—although of course, it takes longer and is more gradual than that—all the rough surfaces give way to the polish and slip of language. Then it can easily seem that the force is in the language, not in the awkward experience it voices. In that initial excitement, when the stanza takes shape for the first time, when the rhyme fits or the cadence has a real music, more poets are lost than found. The temptation is to honor the power of poetry and forget that hinterland where you lived for so long, without a sound in your throat, without a syllable at your command.

I was now seventeen. There was a peculiar indignity for me in the silence of my childhood. Not only had it lacked words; it had lacked a name. When I stood on Hyde Park Corner on my way to school, there was nothing I could put my own idiom on. No slowness of a bus, or blunt corner teashop, or graveyard glimpsed from a train—none of the sights which become the shorthand of a place. Lacking an idiom, I had lacked a place. Therefore, in some strange way, although I talked too much and was a youngest child, I had been silent. Then slowly, in my early adolescence, came the consciousness of poetry. I remembered lines; I came on descriptions. I discovered Yeats and read him. Then, inching my way forward again, I began to make literary idioms, however self-conscious and artificial, for the color of the Liffey and the swans on it. It was awkward and sentimental, but it fitted words to the place for the first time.

Now, in my eighteenth year, I had gone forward again.
I read more; I became more ambitious. The swans and the
river were woven into something which reached further. All
at once I became aware of the real power in form. The poems
I wrote were still forced, but the act of writing them became
less so.

At night I went up to the small dormitory above the bay.
The evenings were less cold and growing longer. I might still
see the eucalyptus tree in the last light. The sky stayed bright
over the evergreens, and I could hear a bell from a church
over to the east. The clarity of color and sound added to my
feeling of power. And so without warning, and in that particular loneliness which is almost inseparable from the dangerous
growth of understanding, I came to know the rewards and
jubilance of control. I learned how to write a line with a ringing sound. I learned a a small amount about the paragraph of
the stanza. The river grew more elegant, the swans more important, and considerably less real. I sat there night after night
writing—putting down words and crossing them out. Gradually I gained control. Gradually I erased Rilke's question: "Go
inside yourself. Discover the motive that bids you write; ex-
amine whether it sends its roots down to the deepest places of
your heart, confess to yourself whether you would have to die
if writing were denied you. This before all: ask yourself in the
quietest hour of your night: *must* I write?"

I wore a school uniform, which was dark green, with a
flannel shirt and a heavy sweater. The dark woolen cuff on
my right wrist was always under my eye as I turned the page.

I came to know its threads, the weave and texture of the way the shirt cuff was turned under it.

By now I was reading Latin literature. The Sixth Book of the *Aeneid*. Day by day the lines accumulated. It was a slow magic, an incantation of images and structures, a pounding syntax. The story line was clear and uncomplicated. Aeneas, Virgil's hero, has already traveled through other lands in other books. He has courted and betrayed Dido in Carthage. He has left her to commit suicide and sailed with the Trojan fleet to Libya and on to Sicily. Now the Sixth Book opens, and Aeneas visits the Cumaean sibyl in Italy. Once he has got the Golden Bough, she descends with him to the underworld and to the river Styx, and on the far shore of it they see the dead.

♦ ♦ ♦

Let me look back again. The table is round and drab; the worn linen stays on the armrests; the sky is full of the light and danger of spring. The same gulls. The same pupils walking and laughing below the window, the same slight and irritating grinding where they walk on the gravel. The usual text is spread out, creased at the edges.

What my second sight shows me is not about the room, or the action, but about myself. I see, as I bend over the page, that everything which has defined my life up to that moment is something which has not happened. I have not had an Irish childhood. I have not found my sexuality. I feel no casual ownership about the distances behind me. My sense of language, therefore, is of something powerful enough to keep me sexless and stateless. In that realm I feel my wants and absences least. In this language, most of all, with its syntax, its complete and structured perceptions there are no small spaces for a childhood, an exile, to get through. These paragraphs are barricades against regret and anxiety. I can read them, day after day, as armories.

♦ ♦ ♦

The poet's vocation—or, more precisely, the historical construction put upon it—is one of the single, most problematic areas for any woman who comes to the craft. Not only has it been defined by a tradition which could never foresee her, but it is construed by men about men, in ways which are poignant, compelling and exclusive.

For instance, I understood, even then, the charm of Gosse's description of Swinburne: "He sat back in the deep sofa in his sitting room, his little feet close together, his arms against his side, folded in his frock-coat like a grasshopper in its wing-covers, and fallen asleep apparently for the night before I could blow out the candles and steal forth from the door."

But charming as it was, the description was of a piece with the exclusiveness. I looked with care and interest at the sketch of Keats in his death sweat, of Shelley with his shirt collar undone. They moved and interested me. I could feel the enticement to feel like that, to develop some precocious maleness which would carry me towards it.

And there was another tradition, encoded in the lost language of a nation which I was just beginning to sense somewhere beyond that schoolroom. A land of wounds. Of scalded flesh and a single God. Where a complex and vital relation had existed between poetry and faith, between the vocation of the poet and the demands of a society. If the boy poet was the image of the British tradition, the bardic poet was the shadow left on the Irish one.

"The Gaelic social order in Ireland," writes the scholar James Carney, "lasted from centuries before the beginnings of recorded history into the seventeenth century. It was in many ways an archaic society the origin of whose institutions are to be sought in the remote period of Indo-European unity. In this society the composing of poetry was not the occupation of the specially gifted, the aesthete or the dilettante. Poetry, even in Christian times, partook of the nature of a religious institution and was so closely woven into the fabric of political Gaeldom that without it that society could not continue to exist unless by changing its political essence."

The paradox of those traditions, with their sense of exclusiveness, was that I saw the power of language more clearly. I sensed a force that could heal wounds and soothe indecision. In the great systems of syntax I was just beginning to understand and in the faltering poems I wrote in the last light, I found a temptation to look for that place between the words themselves where I could forget girlhood and its longing, forget the dislocation of a childhood, clothe myself in an old and inherited sense of possession and so divide myself from the frailties which so far were all I knew of my self.

At one level, I sat at a table with a spring tide behind me and learned a lesson. At another, the lessons I was learning were about powerlessness and not power. My body betrayed me into all the conventional dreams of girlhood. The Victorian hero glowed out of the novels I studied, signaling the peace of submission and belonging. But the country I belonged to offered no ready answers and no predictable destiny. By day I read Latin; at night I read Yeats and tried to write my own poetry. By day I touched the granite and marble of words. At nighttime I followed language into a land of hurt and disappointment.

My knowledge of Irish history was sketchy and still incomplete. But I understood enough to sense the rage and anxiety of a long nineteenth-century hunt for a place. What was harder to place was my own body and mind, caught in the sunny nowhereish morning of a schoolroom, learning the language of conquest in a country which had known nothing else. And as I bent over the page, every one of those anomalies came with me.

♦ ♦ ♦

That moment of discovery and power is so dangerous for the developing poet because it marks the point at which he or she stumbles on one of the family secrets of the tradition. That secret in turn was whispered throughout the nineteenth century, when, with the breakdown of faith and

certainty, a new portrayal of the imagination became commonplace: the imagination as sacramental force, as a laying on
of hands. The argument gained strength as organized religion
declined. In his Oxford lectures on poetry Matthew Arnold
said:

> There is not a creed which is not shaken, not an accredited
> dogma which is not shown to be questionable, not a re-
> ceived tradition which does not threaten to dissolve. Our
> religion has materialised itself in the fact, in the supposed
> fact; it has attached its emotion to the fact and now the fact
> is failing it. But for poetry the idea is everything; the rest is
> a world of illusion, of divine illusion. Poetry attaches its
> emotion to the idea; the idea is the fact. The strongest part
> of our religion today is its unconscious poetry.

I read his words as part of my studies. But they were
beyond me. I was still a teenager in uniform, in the city where
my childhood had not happened, feeling the first power and
confusion of sexuality, dreading that the larger exiles would
follow from the smaller one: that I would suffer the loss of self
after the absence of self. The shaken creeds, the dissolving
traditions I knew were all the local and unimportant ones of
my own history. For that reason, the piercing irony of his
words was lost on me. I did not understand that to invest the
imagination with sacramental powers restores to poetry not its
religious force but its magical function. In the oldest societies
they had been part and parcel of each other. But magic is the
search for control over an unruly environment; it is also the
most inferior of the past associations of poetry. Yet it was

what I rejoiced in as I sat at night, the bay in the distance, making artifice, making music. I did not know that the best such magic could achieve would be a simplification of life based on a dread of it.

I know now that I came to that room, that table, that coastal distance with almost nothing. I had no language and no country. I had no accurate sense of my sexuality, no real knowledge of my imaginative capacity. I was cast in the part of a schoolgirl, with a frayed woolen cuff and a single book. Here in this dead language, which had never been heard on this island, which had never been written for women, I came upon a construct which admitted me through its own sense of power and my longing for it.

I have described it in an incomplete and halting way. Nothing can recover the airless fragrances of the room, the contrast between the space outside and the silence within. The counterpoint between a finished and closed syntax and the unfinished laughter downstairs, the musical sounds of gossip and friendship. Nothing can bring back the exact way my eye fell on the cuff of my sleeve or the first occasion on which I understood the spin and run of a piece of Latin argument.

On the other hand, there is something representative and telling about the moment as I look back at it. At the time it was random and scattered. I came to the room every morning. I sat down. I may have felt the sun gradually warming the room, where before I could have deciphered the frost with my back turned to it. After a few minutes the door would open. My Latin teacher would enter, carrying pencils, a book, a basket, and her scarf tied. She would sit down at right angles and read from separate books.

But now I know that the moment when any poet encounters language, its sheer force and enclosure, is a vital one. In my case I had come from the silences of a childhood which had not happened to a language so closed, so powerful, so exclusive of the doubt of those silences that I looked at it with longing and doubt. For a whole springtime in my seventeenth year I was close to the way a gerund, an ablative, a construction of logic can happen. Until then I had tried nothing but halting poems and unfinished sentences. When I wrote an essay or a poem, I saw the vulnerabilities of language and its exposures. But here was a language which was also a system; here was a code of meaning and arrangement where the mind could be protected from its own frailties.

When the lesson was over, I would take out my exercise book and begin the long, complicated constructions by which every possibility of argument was construed in the Latin way. The spring got louder behind me. The sky softened. Less often now was the frost laid heavily on the grass when I came in. More and more, I saw the polished sentences, the formidable arrangements gather the imperfections of the language I knew and turn it into the language I had learned. More and more often, I saw how to take the unreason of one language and make it safe in the grammar of another. Language as exposure became language as protection.

♦ ♦ ♦

The moment was deep in the Sixth Book. Aeneas has endured the foulness of hell. He has crossed the polished waters, heard the wingbeats of the doves, seen the furious expression on the face of Dido. Now at last he has reached the place where his old companions and rivals in war are clustered. All the names of heroes, the meaningless, difficult Latin names, are recorded at this point. Glaucus. Medon. Thersilichus. I hated the names and found them difficult to remember and unlocated in any adventure I understood. And yet here was Aeneas pressing on again, surrounded by old friends, old rivals. The names, the difficulties of the text fell away. Here were his old adversaries, both pleased and terrified to see him, ready to make a run for the ships, but ready also to hail him. But as they did, the moment happened: They raised *exiguam vocem*—a feeble voice. In the words of the Latin, the cry they attempted mocked them.

I understood. This underworld, with its branches, its rituals, its foul water and difficult names, was a place after all. It was not exactly its furnishings that caught my eye. No seventeen-year-old takes easily to such artifice, with its three-headed ghost, its personifications of War and Famine, its dark bullocks and saucers of blood. Nevertheless, for one moment on an April day it became continuous with the gulls screaming and dipping, the evergreens and the metallic gleam of sea.

For that moment I could make a single experience out of the fractures of language, country and womanhood that had brought me here. The old place of power and heroism—the stairs and bricks of an alien building, the sting of exile—were gathered into a hell with old inscriptions and immediate force.

In the face of that underworld, and by the force of poetry itself, language had been shown to be fallible. The heroes had spoken, and their voices had not carried. Memory was a whisper, a sound that died in your throat. Amidst the triumphs of language and civilization it was a moment of sheer powerlessness. It was something I would look back to when I became a poet.

5.

TURNING AWAY

At nineteen years of age I was a poet; I was sure of it. Now I look back I see the assurance itself as flawed and callow. But at the time it seemed enough. I lived in a small flat looking out on a busy road. I wore a skirt and a woolen jumper and a raincoat on wet days, and felt nothing about them. I had little enough interest in clothes. But the rooms of the flat had personalities. They welcomed or resisted me, and some part of me opened or closed in them. One faced north towards a convent balcony where a nun in a wimple and black habit walked slowly up and down at sunset. Another looked out on a garden with a crooked path. Occasionally a boy would come back with me, at the end of a college day, and we would lie on the floor or in the bed, caught in an odd unhappening dream of pleasure or hope. But rarely. It was language and not sex that happened there.

I had a soft and angry way of writing a poem. I would take a copy book and a biro, set it down on a table and make a jug of milky coffee. I would sit there, as if beside someone with a fever, waiting for the lines, the figures, the forms to take shape. I wrote it down and crossed it out; I read it out loud and wrote it again. I made it better. I made it worse.

I had a sense of language and a preliminary sense of form. I knew, in a poor sort of way, that this human action of sitting in a chair, taking a pen, writing lines on a page was part of the history of the poem. In one way I was right. That action of closing the fingers of my right hand around a pen, of marking the page—there, alone in that small room—was indeed the central act; by this, the poem and its history happened at one and the same time. What I lacked was a clear or useful sense of how this central statement, by its very occurrence, touched and disordered all the other statements.

◆　◆　◆

The city I could reach by a five- or six-minute bus ride was the location of an odd and powerful moment of European poetry. On the surface such literary life as it had was

limited to a few coffeehouses and pubs. The pubs were
crowded and badly lit. Sometimes they had old-fashioned and
plumped-out seats, running against the wall, under mirrors
engraved with the names of whiskeys or distilleries. Then it
was possible to sit back in an atmosphere of noise and smoke,
watching the glitter and crush of the evening happening in
the mirrors.

It was not the substance of the conversation which drew
me to those places—too much of it was gossip—but the shape
of the conversation was different. At first the literary surface
was an ordinary mix of information and malice. As such it was
the replica of all such conversations which hover around the
subject of success or failure. So-and-so had a book out. It was
good; it was not good. He had been paid. Or much more
likely, he had not been paid. More whiskeys. More details.

But if you listened carefully, as the night went on, you
could hear an older historiography at work. The man—it was
always a man—who was considered to have written good poetry was spoken of, if only for a bare moment, as exempt from
the routine, scathing criticism. The poet described in that way
was respected as a man who had put his fields, his enemies, his
townlands into the poem. Who had brought his own reality
to the poem and to whom the poem had yielded. For that
moment he ceased to be described in terms of success and was
talked about, although often so quickly you had to listen carefully, in terms of power.

The name I heard most often was that of Patrick Kavanagh. He had come to Dublin from a border farm a quarter

century before, in the impossible aftermath of the Literary
Revival. An awkward, sometimes fierce countryman, he had
revealed the hypocrisies and costs of a national literature. In
the fifties, sick and disaffected in the aftermath of a wounding
libel case, he would sit on a bench beside the canal, the same
ordinary piece of water that was near my flat. And there, with
no word about nation or history, he had staked a claim to a
new piece of ground. "O commemorate me where there is
water."

For all this, apart from that elusive undertone of respect,
there was nothing reverent in the talk about him; on the contrary. References to him were always familiar and sometimes,
since he was not an easy man, exasperated. Yet from those
conversations I took away a clear inference. Yeats had made a
literature. Kavanagh had made the single, daring act of protest
which pointed the way forward.

◆ ◆ ◆

When closing time came, I was not far from home. I
never drank, and so I came out clearheaded and on the edge
of enchantment. I would walk home or take the last bus, my
mind full of names and fragments of information. The cool,
splashy darkness of a spring or autumn night would go by.
Then I would turn the key and climb the stairs to my flat and
find there the notebook still open on the oilskin tablecloth
and the window with a few stars stuck to it.

I had no words for it, no way of structuring perception
and no one to structure it for me. Yet I was beginning to

understand that the marks on the page were a fraction of an inch high but reached a hundred miles deep into a country's past; its fears, superstitions and memories.

The conversations I had heard were part of it. They were not elegant or well judged, those conversations. But in their way they were firsthand evidence that in this city two powerful histories of the European poem met and merged. The first was the history of the metropolitan poem, which had increasingly detached itself from powers and princes and had, with the romantic movement, become the commanding text of an interior life. Dublin with its Georgian squares, its fanlights and candle sconces was no stranger to this poem which had crossed the sea to it in the nineteenth century and had been heard in drawing rooms and recited in vicarages. It proposed, at its weakest, only a fiction of inwardness. And as such it was a fashionable accessory for young women and the men who wished to please them. At its best it offered a rare and unsettling glimpse of an inner landscape.

The other history, the other poem, was different. It was both sharper and more bitter, as well as more concerned with the external meaning of a poet's life. It was the history of the bard, the prince's friend, the honored singer. Who made his way from village to village, shifting from praise to invective as the occasion demanded. Who celebrated christenings and weddings, who flattered his patrons and excoriated their enemies. Who became, reluctantly, a witness to the totality of the British conquest and the loss of a vital language. After a childhood away, I did not speak that language. But I sensed that the poem it remembered was as deep in Irish life as the other was an outcome of British civilization. It was scarred by its origins and made loud by injustice. It gave a wider role to the poet and more credence to his prince.

◆ ◆ ◆

For many years I could make little sense of it—this remembered image of a girl in a jumper and skirt, leaving her flat, climbing onto the open, rocking platform of a bus and going into the heart of a city. For years, pieces of the journey and the destination would come back to me, like missing sections of a photograph. The curve and sway of the bus as it turned by Stephen's Green, and the trees to one side of the road. The smoky interior of a pub, a glass of stout on the table, with a broken creamy top and someone arguing about poetry. I remember the conversations with other poets and a growing estrangement from all kinds of assumptions which seemed easily or readily available to them. And then back to the flat. To the tablecloth. To the page.

It is there I now see myself. The window I am sitting against is an iron-framed square, small enough, and giving on a garden with an apple tree and a crooked path. The winter light is just sufficient to show me the marks which have been written. I know some things, even as I look back now. I know that my poem, poor as it looks on the page, has good intentions. It wants to say all the ambiguities, awkward regrets and distances of my childhood. It wants to say a country in which some strangeness of relation keeps happening, so that I am drawn in and unassimilated at the same time. It wants to unsay the cadences and certainties of one kind of Irishness. What the girl, whose face is absorbed and turned away, does not know yet is that these are radical acts. They will not be enabled because of some grace of expression or a stumbled-over eloquence on a winter evening. They will require a series of engagements and assessments with the place and the time and the poem. They will require a sense of location in these, and then an act of leave-taking.

◆ ◆ ◆

But for now the city, with its twilights and meeting places, its conversations and memories, seemed made for poetry. There was even an enchantment about it. At night, after hours of rain, the pavements had the look of wet coal. The air in a café or a pub would be warm with the wrung-out smell of wet tea cloths. There was something about the impermanence of a table with empty glasses, or a cigarette turning itself into a sculpture of ash, which suggested the small melodrama of homelessness. On a given night everyone at that table, everyone with a glass or a cigarette—I was sure of it—secretly wanted to be a poet.

Here, if anywhere, I should be able to take up the poetic existence which was apparently on offer in this place. It was set out as a series of hopeful tensions: between bard and poet maudit. Between eighteenth-century mandarin and nineteenth-century romantic. It even seemed to me sometimes that I experienced one version or other of the poet according to which direction I took in the morning. If I got off the bus and continued into Trinity College, I was back in the country of Goldsmith and Burke. On my way to lectures I could, if such a thing were possible, have reached out a hand and touched the preromantic scholarly poem. I could have climbed a stairway in any of the buildings in Front Square and walked back two centuries into a room as close and dark, as sheltered by cherry trees and quadrangles as the one in which Thomas Gray wrote his "Elegy in a Country Churchyard." Everything reminded me that I was in a place of civility and reason. Even the cobblestones at the end of the day—small lumps of moonlight as I walked towards the city—recalled it.

But if I started out for Grafton Street, for a café or a pub, then sooner or later I would catch sight of something different: older and harder to see, but just as powerful. Not exactly a tradition. And nothing as formed as an aesthetic. But a living stream of talk, for all that, which recognized the poem in its time, which was angry and forceful and believing. On certain nights it was even possible to imagine its link to a lost world of Irish poetry, a place where the Irish bard Aodghan O'Rathaille had seen the Gaelic order collapse and his own patrons flee after the Treaty of Limerick failed at the end of the seventeenth century, and where he had been maddened by grief and pride into political poems, even while he was reduced to eating periwinkles on the Atlantic shore of Kerry.

Here in this city, itself caught between definitions, the concept of the poet should have been a rich and powerful one. There were even moments, such as those late-night conversations in the pubs, when a zone of grace opened for a moment and one tradition laid a hand on the other's shoulder.

In the eighteenth century, for instance, Oliver Goldsmith—a young poet, struggling between medicine and literature—had moved around London, among the epigrams and coffeehouses of a sophisticated city, in the age of science, of skepticism, of reason. For all the enclosure and self-regard of Augustan London, he had been able to recognize and salute the older and darker version of the poet.

"Their bards in particular," he wrote of the Irish, "are still held in great veneration among them: those traditionary heralds are invited to every funeral, in order to fill up the interval of the howls with their songs and harps. In these they rehearse the actions of the ancestors of the deceased, bewail the bondage of their country under the English government and generally conclude with advising the young men and maidens to make the best use of their time, for they will soon, for all their present bloom, be stretched under the table, like the dead body before them."

But I was still a teenager. Freckle-faced and bookish, anxious to take a protective coloring from this sharp-edged world I had found. In my struggle to find a life, I took for granted the wealth of ambiguity around me. And so I got up in the morning, put the silvery kettle on the gas ring and made a cup of instant coffee. Then took a bus to whichever station allowed me to look, half conscious and half aware, into the fierce countenance of Irish history.

I was deliberately lonely. I liked the edgy solitude of nighttime walks which never took me far—perhaps only a round or so of the Green, under the streetlamps. Or the less than half mile from the Green to my flat. I liked spending time on my own over a cup of coffee, looking out on a street. I discovered there was something familiar and consoling about urban shapes: a vista of umbrellas or an infantry of feet moving towards a traffic light.

I look back now and I see that solitude as a forcing house of perception, as nurturing a growing unease. I was still short of the exact words, the accurate perceptions. I still talked at night, and listened, with real excitement. And yet I was beginning to feel oddly stranded. Something was obstructing me, throwing me off course. I was between a poem—there, at home, on the tablecloth—and an idea of the poet. I could control the poem, even though it was with half-learned and hand-to-mouth techniques. I could listen for, and understand, the idea of the poet I picked up at night in the conversations I heard around me. But the space between them filled me with an odd malaise. Something about it seemed almost to have the force of an exclusion order.

Sometimes on my way to college, or making a detour to have a cup of coffee in the morning, I saw my reflection in a shopwindow. I never liked what I saw. A redheaded girl, always self-conscious, never graceful enough. I saw the middle height, the untidiness, even the freckles if I went up close. I saw the student, the daughter, the girl friend, the bad-tempered fifth child. It was a measure of the confusion I felt, the increasing drain on my purpose and clearheadedness that I hardly ever thought I saw an Irish poet.

♦ ♦ ♦

I met Patrick Kavanagh in a café at the end of Grafton Street in Dublin. It was the middle sixties. He was within two years or so of his death. I sat at a small table, facing the door which opened out onto the street. I could see shop fronts and passersby. He sat with his back to the street: a man in early old age, wearing a coat and spectacles and a soft felt hat. I doubt if we talked for more than half an hour, forty minutes at the most.

In a simple sense, he was a man trying to eat his lunch in peace on a winter afternoon. I was callow enough to introduce myself; he was courteous enough to show no surprise and no irritation. I remember some details clearly; others have faded. I remember he wore a soft felt hat at a rakish angle. But his coat will not come clear in my memory. It might have been a gaberdine raincoat. Then again I may have reinvented that from familiar photographs. I do remember that we ate hamburgers, which were then still new in Dublin. They were served on green plastic plates, on a dimpled paper napkin. As Kavanagh spoke—and he was short of breath from a lung operation—the paper fluttered under the hamburger.

His style of speech was shy and apocalyptic. He had a

distinctive register of amazement, and impatience and dismissal. He spoke with real irritation about certain characters, "poetasters," as he would have called them. And shortly afterwards he told me with real pleasure that he had seen a golden eagle—in the States, I think—and that it was followed by "a retinue of little birds." But the connection is mine, not his.

By then Kavanagh had lived in Dublin for more than twenty years. I knew a little about him: that he had left Monaghan at the end of the thirties, that he had come to Dublin in search of literary fellowship. And that he regretted the decision. "No man," he once wrote of his townland, "ever loved that landscape and even some of the people more than I." Dublin, however, was another matter. He had come to the city in the aftermath of the Literary Revival. He was scathing about its rhetoric and its preconceptions. "When I came to Dublin," he had written, "the Irish Literary Affair was still booming. It was the notion that Dublin was a literary metropolis and Ireland as invented and patented by Yeats, Lady Gregory and Synge, a spiritual entity. It was full of writers and poets and I am afraid I thought their work had the Irish quality."

He finished lunch, drank a cup of tea and got up from the table. I stayed behind. The day still had big spaces in it. Nothing about it gave me an inkling—not at this point—that this had been important. Even so, I had touched something which would return to me later: an example of dissidence. Kavanagh was a countryman; I was a woman. Neither of those circumstances had much meaning for the other. But I had seen the witness of someone who had used the occasion of his life to rebuff the expectations and preconceptions of the Irish poem. I would remember it.

◆ ◆ ◆

For all my unease, I was learning. It was a slow process, full of excitements. I was beginning to understand something about the poem on the page. Weekends and late at night I worked at line lengths, stanza lengths, rhyme schemes.

I began to revel in it. The growth of control over language is one of the true—and one of the most deceptive—rewards for a young poet. There was less disappointment now as I sat at the table by the window. I was beginning also to connect my reading with my writing. The history of the stanza and the line was no longer abstract. At times, when something came out right on the page in front of me, or at least seemed to, a limitless adventure of language seemed to open backwards, like a map with trade routes offering access to only a few in every generation.

It was a solemn and self-conscious way of doing things, and yet the elements of form were still important in the Irish poem. They held it in place and pinned it down. It never occurred to me, at that point anyway, to question it. To that extent I was working on the received version of a poem, and my real achievement would be not a perfection of style or stanza but a growing doubt. In the meantime, on those dark, enclosed nights, in the odd loneliness and emptiness of a late girlhood, I labored over someone else's poem. I was dogged about it. The telephone would ring. Friends would arrange a meeting. I would answer the phone and accept the invitation. But I always came back to the window, to the table, to the page. Once the young brother of a friend, a boy of about sixteen, called as I was finishing a poem that seemed important at the time. It was an afternoon in March. The garden outside was full of cold beginnings. The first blossoms. The last daffodils. A thrush calling. He looked at me, tongue-tied and round-cheeked, across the table. My copybook was open; the marks were on the page, waiting to be added to. For just a moment I felt the strangeness of it all. The stilted talk; the task that never ended. Then it passed, and I was impatient for him to go.

It was an illusion—I learned that later—this sense of the enclosure and isolation of the work. But every young poet yields to it. It gives a glamour to the rented room and the painted blue dresser. It makes the window with its stars and leaves seem the edge and not the end of possibility. It turns an act of language into a sense of power.

♦ ♦ ♦

Poetry as magic. Every young poet, struggling to find words, sooner or later touches that old and superstitious idea. Every apprentice, however clumsy with a piece of meter or a paragraph of music, has a sense—if only for a moment—that to name the lightning is to own it.

I felt it also. But in an oblique and surprising way. Because I was starting to locate myself in language, I was slowly, after so many disappointments, beginning to find myself in place. Gradually the city was catching my attention. Not far from my flat was the canal. At night the water glittered under streetlamps, the grass of the towpath took on a livid color and the wooden bulk of the locks turned into hunches of shadow.

Patrick Kavanagh had come here in the mid-fifties. He had sat by the water within sight of the bridge and the traffic. There was nothing particularly beautiful about the spot he had chosen. It was a noisy inch of city, shadowed by poplars and intruded on by passersby. He had been a sick man then, disillusioned and estranged. And with his foot on that inch, he had written a visionary sonnet. I never passed the canal at that point without thinking of it. *O commemorate me where there is water.* There was something so downright and local about the poem that it opened out, for the first time, the idea of place as something language could claim even if ownership had been denied.

Language. Ownership. My childhood had been tormented by those fractions. The absence of my own place had led to the drying up of my own language. The shorthand of possession, the inherited nicknames for a sweetshop or a dead tree or a public house on the site of a well—I understood now that they could not happen because the inheritance had not happened.

After midnight the city was quiet. I wore high heels, tipped with steel. I could hear them clicking and ringing as I set out for home. My flat was near enough to Stephen's Green to make it a short walk, and a safe one. It was not stone or

water which moved me as I went along, nor light, nor even
the combination of it all. It was the recurrences: the same
granite rise of the bridge at Baggot Street, the same pear tree
at the top of Waterloo Road. The same tree stump, waist-
high, as you turned into Morehampton Road. A few more
minutes and I came to the railed front gardens of the half
street where I lived. My flat was at the top. I could see the
window of my bedroom, the light I had forgotten to turn out,
the shape of the roof which made the ceiling slope. By the
time I reached the front door I would be fluent in streetlamps
and the color of iron under them. I would know that the
copybook waited for me, and the pen. And I was full of the
new knowledge that language can reclaim location.

◆ ◆ ◆

My solitude was an illusion. No poet, however young or
disaffected, writes alone. It is a connected act. The words on
the page, though they may appear free and improvised, are on
hire. They are owned by a complicated and interwoven past
of language, history, happenstance.

The moment I was in was complicated enough. Ireland
was emerging from two decades of airless self-reflection. I had
been born in one of them, and not far from the flat I was
writing in. I could have gone out of my door, turned left and
walked for half a mile. I would have come to a broad street of
set-back, well-built houses. They had railings at the front and
a flight of steps to the front door. One of them, my old house,
had a lilac bush right up against the railings. Even now I re-

membered the cloying, sweetish residue of lilac under my fingernails.

I never walked that half mile. It was, despite the actual nearness, an impossible distance. I had left there at five years of age. I was the sum of all the contradictions and interruptions which had divided me from the childhood I might have had. A clear line of identity had been broken. I had a flawed sense of the immediate past. I had spent the fifties, a crucial decade, outside the country. The religious festivals, the Irish dancing, the political meetings—they were missing from my vocabulary. I had not relearned them; I hardly knew they were missing. I sat down to write the Irish lyric with no sense of ownership, no automatic feeling of access.

The lyric I wrote had its own past and a stubborn series of contradictions which I discovered with my own. It had come with difficulty out of the claims and counterclaims made on it by the previous half century. Its currency represented both a survival and a compromise. Despite Yeats's example, the poetic model I encountered in Dublin was nearer to Joyce's quatrain, and its pre-Raphaelite influence, than the modernist paragraph, bristling with syntax and argument, which Yeats had used. The stanza I wrote, almost without thinking, was a hybrid: half British movement poem and half Irish lyric. Both had their roots in a Victorian romanticism, where the movement from stanza to stanza had a soft music about it.

Somewhere further back, I would sense this later, those poems split apart. The Irish poem continued traveling back into the rough angers of the street ballad, into the music and anxiety of a nationalist song. And further back again into the folk memory of bardic purpose and invective. The British poem tensed into the rearrangements of the true romantic movement, with its radical proposals about an inner and outer world.

◆ ◆ ◆

It is late at night. The room is airless and warm. The overhead light is on, and the coffee jug is empty. I am just a few days short of my twentieth birthday. When I sit down to write, I have an uncanny sense of spoiled identity and uncertain origin. I start to write about a swan. It is a legendary image at first, cloaked in the resonance of a myth. I try the stanzas, the structures. I write down nouns and adjectives, relishing the distance of this swan from the dirty, clustered birds I have seen at the foot of a bridge on the Liffey. Then the line falters. I try again. This time the swan in the poem is neither close to the birds at the foot of the bridge nor part of a convincing myth. I try again.

Finally, only when most of what I write has been scrapped, I see the image for what it is. I see a swan that has never been imagined, only received. That has never been part of an Irish myth or a true legend. That has come in fact, as one of the doubtful gifts of "The Victorian Gael"—an image from some declining part of a colonial tradition, smuggled from British drawing rooms into Irish poems. And so, on an ordinary evening in a city, bent over a copybook, and writing nothing of any importance, I have felt under my pen the flurry and corruption of divided language: a grammar of imagination split from top to bottom.

II.

At first it was nothing. Just a dissonance glimpsed out of the corner of my eye, sensed in a solitude of coffee cups and mid-city mornings. Just one part of a larger unease. Then it grew wider and more puzzling: this sense of a gap between one part of me which wrote poetry and one part of me which did not.

There were times when I felt like a poet, and times when I did not. I felt like a poet in the kitchen of the flat. There, with the coffee mug and my copybook, I was equal to the definition. There, where no one could see me, I found parts of myself which only that strange working and reworking made visible. A lost mathematician in me saw the numbers in the words and heard the stresses in the line. I was less inclined now to take the inherited image file of the Literary Revival. I began to test the figures in the poem, to look for what was fresh and demanding in the arrangement of the lines.

I chose my skirts more carefully and looked at lipstick colors with interest. One day in a chemist's shop I heard someone talk about the blue tones in a certain shade of it. I waited behind, holding the lipstick up to a small mirror, looking for an elusive blue in the oily cyclamen color, failing to find it. I was twenty years of age now. Able to fall in love, and out again. Able to sit quarreling with boyfriends, crying tears of temper and pride in the same cafés where a year ago I had talked about nothing but poetry.

The differences between myself and the male poets I knew were more obvious now. I felt less at ease, less equal in conversations with them, as if there had been a shift or a rebalancing. I began to notice certain things. If one of these male poets kissed a girl, the kiss would undergo a quick metamorphosis. It would be warm and impulsive one week. The next it would appear collected and purposeful, caught in a cold way between syntax and the metaphor and knowing its place in a sonnet or a villanelle.

My kisses did not appear in my poems. I did not feel like a poet when I kissed a boy. When I went home to my flat, where I did feel like one, the two fractions failed to connect. The part which had learned to be itself because it had found itself in form, which moved a stress back in a line, or split a caesura neatly, the way I had seen my mother split a chicken carcass right down the middle, held aloof from the other part. Obstinately it remained sexless. It could not be heard in some region where a lipstick was held up to a mirror, or a boy caught me by surprise with a kiss. Increasingly it seemed that the power I felt when I wrote a poem came from an avoidance, and not a resolution, of the powerlessness I felt in other ways. No matter what I did, the gap widened.

I talked less about the past than other poets. The figures from it, in their Victorian coats and turned-up silk collars, were too whole and too male. Their lives, at least according to the legends which had survived them, never seemed to have broken apart in the small and ordinary ways mine did.

Yet I loved the poems of that past. Increasingly I had a sense of their force and effect, of the figure they made in the time they were able to rearrange and heal. The more I wrote my own poems, the more I wondered at these other ones. And the more the isolation I felt deepened.

The first enchantment with the city—with its talk, with its casual assumption of a literary destiny—was fading. Once I had come back to the flat, from a day in the library or a night of heady talk, relishing the bus ride, the abrupt stop, the short walk to the gate. It had been enough for me to come up the short flight of steps, turn on the heater, make coffee and sit down at the table. Everything would be as I had left it. The ugly roses on the coffee jug. The cast-iron door of the stove. The red weave on the cover of the copybook. And there, as I had left it also, was the sense of power in a secret language, ready to be taken up again. Yet now I hesitated.

♦ ♦ ♦

The sexuality of any young poet is mysterious. It is not exactly the same thing as the longing for pleasure or the forth-right dreams and disappointments of everyday life. I had those as well. But this was different. It was something to do with a blurred text of names and customs rather than parts of the body or the way some boy turned around on a street corner.

In some complex way I felt—again I am making my ideas more sophisticated in retrospect than they could have been at the time—that the sexuality I could have as a poet was controlled in a way in which that day-to-day, ordinary sexuality was not. That it was allowed rather than spontaneous. It came to be a strange and awkward sense of not having the required permission. I had that sense most when I talked to male poets; I had it increasingly when I opened a book of poetry. Every day, in lectures and tutorials, and then later over coffee and conversation, the names whirled by: Chatterton. Keats. Byron. And the more they passed by me, the less easy I became.

Gradually I began to feel that the poetic tradition itself was a house which held out an uncertain welcome to me. And when I entered it—I am carrying an image forward now as I never would have then—it was as if one room remained shut, locked against the air and intrusion of newness. When the door opened, what was inside was the room of a boy child: everything kept still and poised to enact memory and reverence. His words, his toys all kept in the one place and the one order. Poetic tradition revered the boy child who had so often in its history given it glamour and purpose. It knew—if you can personify a body of opinion and grant it intelligent life—that poets are flawed and grow old, that they compromise with circumstance and are limited by dailyness. But in the intense light falling on a page of poetry, the confusion of those elements of youth and expression gave a venerable craft the poignance it required.

I understood the glamour. I saw the power in those lives which had been lived close to language. I also saw, again in a mute and unconfident way, the cost of such a hallowing of

youth, promise, boyhood. The obvious gain was to a nineteenth-century myth of inspiration, a dearly held belief about
the origins of poetry. The cost was to the poet like myself,
whose mind was welcome in the tradition, but whose body
was a strange and unrecorded part of it. Not strange and unrecorded, that is, if you were the object of the poem. Then
you wore silks and listened to the cadences of the poem and
became the silence they were addressed to. But unrecorded if,
like me, the body you had was drawing you to the life you
would lead.

Nothing I saw in the tradition—not the poems I read on
the page or the conversations I heard from male contempo-
raries—encouraged me to follow my body with my mind and
take myself to a place where they could heal in language: in
new poems, in radical explorations. On the contrary. There
was a deep suspicion of the ordinary life. It was assumed to be
a narrow and antipoetic one.

There was a reason for this. For more than a century the
poet's life had been edging away from the life lived in houses,
parishes, settled communities. It had been fed on a strange
and, finally, damaging self-regard. It was assumed—at least in
the narrow world I knew—that in some way the poet's life
was the highest expression of individuality. That it would
treat only occasionally, and then high-handedly, with the collective systems of a particular time.

Increasingly I doubted all this. The first delight of those
conversations where the poet was exalted, and history made
to sound like his accessory, was wearing off. I read more po-

etry now and not less. I noticed in it things no one spoke of. I saw, in the best of it, a perception of powerlessness and therefore a true understanding of the power of language. But I kept it to myself. If poetry was a kingdom where the boy child was the favored one, where the single human being was elevated to an emblem for all, then I could not live there. And that I hardly wanted to think about.

I walked more at night. The city was safe and almost empty after eleven o'clock. I would come to Stephen's Green and begin a slow, purposeless round of the railings there. The streetlamps threw a yellowish glare on the pavements and benches. The overhanging leaves seemed six inches closer than in daylight. Overhead the sky was violet-colored and cloudy. I did not understand my life. It was, increasingly, a series of places and purposes I had failed to find. A childhood. A country. And now the suspicion was growing in my mind that I would not find a language either. Unformed as I was, anxious as I was to find a home, the ironies were clear to me. Other poets in other countries—and several I knew in this one—had found their way. I had not. In the middle of an emblematic nation, at the heart of a formidable tradition of writing, I was lost.

♦ ♦ ♦

In that year—among the excitements of language and my own suppressed unease—came news of a woman's death. Sylvia Plath, an American poet and only just into her thirties, had died in London. It was a year later again that I began to hear about her. She was talked about in fragments. As a wife. As a suicide. In the heartless asides which pass for neighborly gossip among young poets. Only a few of her later poems were in circulation. It would be another year or so before *Ariel* came out, before the strength of her voice arrived to disrupt the voyeurism about her death.

I began to listen for her name. Information was scarce. It was rare, in any case, that she was spoken about kindly or completely. In such talk as there was about her work and her death I began to notice the same fractures I was starting to find in the attitudes around me to women and poetry. In her case they were intensified. She was a woman here. And a poet there. Weak in this place. Strong in that.

One night, by chance, I heard the date of her death. February 11, 1963. I thought back. I had been eighteen then, and just eight months out of school, living in a basement flat with my sister. The bedroom had backed onto a garden with a line of paving which zigzagged by front trees and chicken wire to the Dodder River.

It was the coldest winter on record since the freeze-up of 1947. The granite windowsill smoked with ice. Milk froze on the doorstep. The twelve steps down to the front door were little rinks in the dark. Every night when we went to bed, our frosty breaths fogged the conversation, while we lay under the covers watching the dish and curve of the electric fire, the two rods which burned dust and glowed. Every morning the clothes on the washing line were splayed into a wild stiffness by frost.

She had died alone in that season. The more I heard, the more pity I felt for it, that single act of desolation. From now on I would write, at least partly, in the shadow of that act: unsettled and loyal. Other poets—men—moved easily among the models of the poet's life, picking and choosing. I chose this one—not to emulate but to honor. Not simply for the beautiful, striving language of the poems when I came to read them. But because I could see increasingly the stresses and fractures between a poet's life and a woman's. And how—alone, at a heartbroken moment—they might become fatal.

◆　◆　◆

But things were changing. I had written my first real poems in this flat, copying them out laboriously while the seasons circled one another outside the window. I had known the excitement of managing my first true piece of syntax, the first cadence that worked. And was still working the next morning. I had practiced here, in self-conscious ways, the poet's outlook. I had gone to bed with poetry in my mind and woken up with it still there. I had seen, arrayed in front of me, on the open page and in my handwriting, the actual elements of magic. I had known that if I found the word for lightning, then lightning was mine.

Now I came back, sat down and felt a shadow across it all. I had learned a language. I had felt its power to control what it expressed. Increasingly I saw there was a price for it.

To have that power, it seemed, I would have to edit

other, less resolved parts of my experience. I could not come to the table, to the copybook, to hold the pen in a certain way, with the bluish lipstick in my mind. Or with an Irishness which was not bardic or historic but full of silences. I could give a voice to the certainties of my mind but not to the questions of my body. Once I had seen myself at that table engaged in the act of history, the work of the poem. Now I saw myself—as if I had stepped outside my body—shriveled and discounted: a woman at a window engaged in a power of language which rebuffed the truth of her life.

The surface was the same. The life of the pubs, the conversations about poetry and among poets, went on as before. But for me now, with a growing sense of unease, they were stateless and unsexed. As the writer of poems I was still a welcome part of them. As a woman I had no place in them. Gradually the anomaly of my poetic existence was clear to me. By luck, or its absence, I had been born in a country where and at a time when the word *woman* and the word *poet* inhabited two separate kingdoms of experience and expression. I could not, it seemed, live in both. As the author of poems I was an equal partner in Irish poetry. As a woman— about to set out on the life which was the passive object of many of those poems—I had no voice. It had been silenced, ironically enough, by the very powers of language I aspired to and honored. By the elements of form I had worked hard to learn.

◆ ◆ ◆

The elements of form. At first they had been part of the costume drama of becoming a poet. I had tackled them in a self-conscious and out-to-please way. In the armed camp that existed after modernism, the Irish poem was something of a neutral zone. Yeats. MacNeice. Kavanagh. They were all vivid and wayward formalists. At the same time, Yeats had reconfigured the Irish poem with different tones and modernist sound effects.

But now, as my doubts increased, even these became part of them. However abstract it looked from outside, the paragraph of language and music was beginning to seem a crucial part of a whole, wider question of identity.

One afternoon, full of wet springtime colors, I knocked on the door of one of the dons at Trinity. He was an elderly man, a patient scholar, well used to intrusions by students. I wanted, I said, to know exactly what form was. I was not a particularly hardworking student, and the question must have seemed to him to come from nowhere. He put his glasses on the desk in front of him. But if he felt surprise, he showed none, and was uncondescending and cautious in his reply. The elements of form, he said, were often inseparable from the factors of external compromise. Think of a play. The three hours of a spatial construct—the stage, the lights, the seating—these influenced even the deepest secrets of the final product.

I walked back across Front Square. The rain had stopped. The cobbles slithered and glanced off a sudden brightness. The plum blossoms were out, and rainwater had

collected at the edges of the pathways. I knew I had heard part
of the truth, well and patiently told. But against the sense of
crisis that was slowly building in my mind, it was not enough.
I walked back down Grafton Street, avoiding places that had
seemed welcoming. I was not a poet—I knew enough to
know this—without a sense of form. But would that sense be
strong enough to stand up to the cracks and fractures which
were starting to overwhelm my whole concept of being a
poet?

I was too young and too muddleheaded to be other than
a derivative technician. But already I knew—from a few mysterious moments of writing—something about form. Already
I sensed that real form—the sort that made time turn and
wander when you read a poem—came from a powerful
meeting between a hidden life and a hidden chance in language. If they found each other, then each could come out of
hiding.

But the hidden life I could offer to such a meeting had
something to do with my sexuality. Not with kisses and lipstick exactly. But with an untidy, unsymmetrical identity that
was somehow bound into the core of my determination and
hope, that was part of my ordinary future as a woman. I knew
so little, and was so divided, that I had already forecast that
future as ordinary. And yet in every conversation I had had
with poets, about poetry, the chance of such a future being a
fit subject for a poem, or a defining lifestyle for a poet, was
subtly discounted. Yet if I were to edit it out—this unformed,

unproved core—I would have nothing to bring to that engagement with language.

◆　◆　◆

Suddenly the making of that sort of form seemed more difficult than I had thought possible. The public forms of Irish poetry—those exterior compromises my teacher had spoken of—now seemed more bleakly exclusive than I had ever thought they would be when I had sat, at nineteen years of age, enchanted by talk about history and bardic purpose. Now even the purposes seemed menacing. They threatened to take away from me my unproved sense of a country and a language and, with them, my own tentative acceptance of the connection between these and my sexuality.

The beautiful place, the land of wounds and recovery, the Ireland of historic interpretation, was becoming, before my eyes, a text in which my name had been written merely to serve and illustrate an object lesson. How could I write it again? It was not only the public forms—those mandates for being a poet and writing a poem—which weighed on me. It was the constant invitation to alter my inner world to make it acceptable to the conventions of the poet which had developed and were sustained all around me. Everywhere I turned there were questions, and everywhere the questions were hard to distinguish from the temptation.

What, for instance, if I chose to engage with language at the level of my apparent life and not my hidden one? What if

I wrote out of the plausible, asexual persona offered to me, obliquely and persuasively, in conversation with other poets? Would it be so wrong to deny a womanhood—an ordinary condition, after all—so as to hold on to this extraordinary privilege of being a young poet? And could I not use the limited entitlements I had, rather than seek out, alone and painfully, ones which were not forthcoming?

But the choices were not real. The truth was simple and terrible. My experience and my powers of expression had broken apart, just as I was learning to put them together. I had come, in a privileged way, to a place where poetry flourished. I had found, in my late teens, what others had failed to find at any time. I had lived in a flat, overlooking a road, with a table and a copybook. And on it had fallen a light of meaning, a powerful beam of traditions and expressions. In that refraction were the gaunt figure and harsh voice of Aodghan O'-Rathaille, reduced to eating periwinkles on the shore in Kerry at the end of the seventeenth century and still convinced of the elaborate posture and claim of the bard. But there also were Clare and Hopkins. And what Yeats had called the meditative pace of the Thames Valley.

I had lived for a short time in this light, feeling it on my hand as I wrote, returning to find it at the end of a day spent among abstractions in a university. And as I wrote, however my words faltered, I had found by that illumination my first, raw sense of the grace and ordeal of becoming a poet.

It was gone. I was now just a twenty-year-old student, climbing the stairs at the end of the day, my books overdue

from the library. The table was still there, the window, the
tablecloth. What was missing was my sense of a poet's life. It
was not there because, finally, I had found it impossible to
accept the strains and divisions it offered. All that remained
was a single, last question. Would I ever find, in the years
ahead of me, that true meeting between a hidden life and a
hidden language out of which true form would come—the
form of a true poem? And after the question, all that was left
was to turn away.

PART TWO

Lessons

6.

Years ago I went to Achill for Easter. I was a student at Trinity then, and I had the loan of a friend's cottage. It was a one-story stone building with two rooms and a view of sloping fields.

April was cold that year. The cottage was in sight of the Atlantic, and at night a bitter, humid wind blew across the shore. By day there was heckling sunshine, but after dark a fire was necessary. The loneliness of the place suited me. My purposes in being there were purgatorial, and I had no intention of going out and about. I had done erratically, to say the least, in my first-year exams. In token of the need to do better, I had brought with me a small, accusing volume of the court poets of the silver age. In other words, those sixteenth-century English songwriters, like Wyatt and Raleigh, whose lines appear so elegant, so offhand yet whose poems smell of the gallows.

I was there less than a week. The cottage had no water, and every evening the caretaker, an old woman who shared a cottage with her brother at the bottom of the field, would carry water up to me. I can see her still. She has a tea towel round her waist—perhaps this is one image that has become all the images I have of her—she wears an old cardigan and her hands are blushing with cold as she puts down the bucket. Sometimes we talk inside the door of the cottage. Once, I remember, we stood there as the dark grew all around us and I could see stars beginning to curve in the stream behind us.

She was the first person to talk to me about the famine. The first person, in fact, to speak to me with any force about the terrible parish of survival and death which the event had been in those regions. She kept repeating to me that they were great people, the people in the famine. *Great people.* I had never heard that before. She pointed out the beauties of the place. But they themselves, I see now, were a subtext. On the eastern side of Keel, the cliffs of Menawn rose sheer out of the water. And here was Keel itself, with its blond strand and broken stone, where the villagers in the famine, she told me, had moved closer to the shore, the better to eat the seaweed.

Memory is treacherous. It confers meanings which are not apparent at the time. I want to say that I understood this woman as emblem and instance of everything I am about to propose. Of course I did not. Yet even then I sensed a power in the encounter. I knew, without having words for it, that she came from a past which affected me. When she pointed out Keel to me that evening when the wind was brisk and cold and the light was going, when she gestured towards that shore which had stones as outlines and monuments of a desperate people, what was she pointing at? A history? A nation? Her memories or mine?

Those questions, once I began to write my own poetry, came back to haunt me. "I have been amazed, more than once," writes Hélène Cixous, "by a description a woman gave me of a world all her own, which she had been secretly haunting since early childhood." As the years passed, my amazement grew. I would see again the spring evening, the woman talking to me. Above all, I would remember how, when I finished speaking to her I went in, lit a fire, took out my book of English court poetry and memorized all over again—with no sense of irony or omission—the cadences of power and despair.

II.

I have written this to probe the virulence and necessity of the idea of a nation. Not on its own and not in a vacuum, but as it intersects with a specific poetic inheritance and as that inheritance, in turn, cut across me as woman and poet. Some of these intersections are personal. Some of them may be painful to remember. Nearly all of them are elusive and difficult to describe with any degree of precision. Nevertheless, I believe these intersections, if I can observe them at all properly here, reveal something about poetry, about nationalism, about the difficulties for a woman poet within a constraining national tradition. Perhaps the argument itself is nothing more than a way of revisiting the cold lights of that western evening and the force of that woman's conversation. In any case, the questions inherent in that encounter remain with me. It could well be that they might appear, even to a sympathetic reader, too complex to admit of an answer. In other words, that an argument like mine must contain too many imponderables to admit of any practical focus.

Yet I have no difficulty in stating the central premise of my argument. It is that over a relatively short time—certainly no more than a generation or so—women have moved from being the objects of Irish poems to being the authors of them. It is a momentous transit. It is also a disruptive one. It raises questions of identity, issues of poetic motive and ethical direction which can seem almost impossibly complex. What is more, such a transit—like the slow course of a star or the shifts in a constellation—is almost invisible to the naked eye. Critics may well miss it or map it inaccurately. Yet such a transit inevitably changes our idea of measurement, of distance, of the past as well as the future. And as it does so, it changes our idea of the Irish poem, of its composition and authority, of its right to appropriate certain themes and make certain fiats.

And since poetry is never local for long, that in turn widens out into further implications.

Everything I am about to argue here could be taken as local and personal, rooted in one country and one poetic inheritance, and both of them mine. Yet if the names were changed, if situations and places were transposed, the issues might well be revealed as less parochial. This is not, after all, an essay on the craft of the art. I am writing not about aesthetics but about the ethics which are altogether less visible in a poetic tradition. Who the poet is, what he or she nominates as a proper theme for poetry, what selves poets discover and confirm through this subject matter—all of this involves an ethical choice. The more volatile the material—and a wounded history, public or private, is always volatile—the more intensely ethical the choice. Poetic ethics are evident and urgent in any culture where tensions between a poet and his or her birthplace are inherited and established. Poets from such cultures might well recognize some of the issues raised here. After all, this is not the only country or the only politic where the previously passive objects of a work of art have, in a relatively short time, become the authors of it.

So it was with me. For this very reason, early on as a poet, certainly in my twenties, I realized that the Irish nation as an existing construct in Irish poetry was not available to me. I would not have been able to articulate it at that point, but at some preliminary level I already knew that the anguish and power of that woman's gesture on Achill, with its suggestive hinterland of pain, were not something I could predict or rely on in Irish poetry. There were glimpses here and there; sometimes more than that. But all too often, when I was searching for such an inclusion, what I found was a rhetoric of imagery which alienated me: a fusion of the national and the feminine which seemed to simplify both.

It was not a comfortable realization. There was nothing clear-cut about my feelings. I had tribal ambivalences and doubts, and even then I had an uneasy sense of the conflict which awaited me. On the one hand, I knew that as a poet I could not easily do without the idea of a nation. Poetry in every time draws on that reserve. On the other, I could not as a woman accept the nation formulated for me by Irish poetry and its traditions. At one point it even looked to me as if the whole thing might be made up of irreconcilable differences. At the very least it seemed to me that I was likely to remain an outsider in my own national literature, cut off from its ar-chive, at a distance from its energy. Unless, that is, I could repossess it. This proposal is about that conflict and that re-possession and about the fact that repossession itself is not a static or single act. Indeed, the argument which describes it may itself be no more than a part of it.

III.

A nation. It is, in some ways, the most fragile and im-probable of concepts. Yet the idea of an Ireland, resolved and healed of its wounds, is an irreducible presence in the Irish past and its literature. In one sense, of course, both the con-cept and its realization resist definition. It is certainly nothing conceived in what Edmund Burke calls "the spirit of rational liberty." When a people have been so dispossessed by event as the Irish in the eighteenth and nineteenth centuries, an extra burden falls on the very idea of a nation. What should be a political aspiration becomes a collective fantasy. The dream itself becomes freighted with invention. The Irish nation, materializing in the songs and ballads of these centuries, is a sequence of improvised images. These songs, these images, wonderful and terrible and memorable as they are, propose for a nation an impossible task: to be at once an archive of defeat and a diagram of victory.

As a child I loved these songs. As a teenager I had sought them out for some meaning, some definition. Even now, in some moods and at certain times, I can find it difficult to resist their makeshift angers. And no wonder. The best of them are written—like the lyrics of Wyatt and Raleigh—within sight of the gibbet. They breathe just free of the noose.

In one sense I was a captive audience. My childhood was spent in London. My image makers as a child, therefore, were refractions of my exile: conversations overheard, memories and visitors. I listened and absorbed. For me, as for many another exile, Ireland was my nation long before it was once again my country. That nation, then and later, was a session of images: of defeats and sacrifices, of individual defiances happening offstage. The songs enhanced the images; the images reinforced the songs. To me they were the soundings of the place I had lost: drowned treasure.

It took me years to shake off those presences. In the end,

though, I did escape. My escape was assisted by the realization that these songs were effect, not cause. They were only the curators of the dream, not the inventors. In retrospect I could accuse both them and the dream of certain crucial simplifications. I made then, as I make now, a moral division between what those songs sought to accomplish and what Irish poetry must seek to achieve. The songs, with their postures and their angers, glamorized resistance, action. But the Irish experience, certainly for the purposes of poetry, was only incidentally about action and resistance. At a far deeper level—and here the Achill woman returns—it was about defeat. The coffin ships, the soup queues, those desperate villagers at the shoreline—these things had actually happened. The songs, persuasive, hypnotic, could wish them away. Poetry could not. Of course, the relation between a poem and a past is never that simple. When I met the Achill woman, I was already a poet, I thought of myself as a poet. Yet nothing that I understood about poetry enabled me to understand her better. Quite the reverse. I turned my back on her in that cold twilight and went to commit to memory the songs and artifices of the very power systems which had made her own memory such an archive of loss.

If I understand her better now, and my relation to her, it is not just because my sense of irony or history has developed over the years, although I hope they have. It is more likely because of my own experience as a poet. Inevitably any account of this carries the risk of subjective codes and impressions. Yet in poetry in particular and women's writing in general, the private witness is often all there is to go on. Since my personal experience as a poet is part of my source material, it is to that I now turn.

IV.

I entered Trinity to study English and Latin. Those were the early sixties, and Dublin was another world—a place for which I can still feel Henry James's "tiger-pounce of home-sickness." In a very real sense it was a city of images and anachronisms. There were still brewery horses on Grafton Street, their rumps draped and smoking under sackcloth. In the coffee bars eggs were poached in a rolling boil and spooned onto thick, crustless toast. The lights went on at twilight; by midnight the city was full of echoes.

After the day's lectures I took a bus home from college. It was a short journey. Home was an attic flat on the near edge of a town that was just beginning to sprawl. There in the kitchen, on an oilskin tablecloth, I wrote my first real poems: derivative, formalist, gesturing poems. I was a very long way from Adrienne Rich's realization that "instead of poems about experience, I am getting poems that are experiences." If anything, my poems were other people's experiences. This, after all, was the heyday of the movement in Britain, and the neat stanza, the well-broken line were the very stuff of poetic identity.

Now I wonder how many young women poets taught themselves—in rooms like that, with a blank discipline—to write the poem that was in the air, rather than the one within their experience? How many faltered, as I did, not for lack of answers but for lack of questions. "It will be a long time still, I think," wrote Virginia Woolf, "before a woman can sit down to write a book without finding a phantom to be slain, a rock to be dashed against."

But for now let me invent a shift of time. I am turning down those streets which echo after midnight. I am climbing the stairs of a coffee bar which stays open late. I know what I will find. Here is the salt-glazed mug on a tabletop which is as scarred as a desk in a country school. Here is the window with its view of an empty street, of lamplight and iron. And there, in the corner, is my younger self.

I draw up a chair, I sit down opposite her. I begin to talk—no, to harangue her. Why, I say, do you do it? Why do you go back to that attic flat, night after night, to write in forms explored and sealed by Englishmen hundreds of years ago? You are Irish. You are a woman. Why do you keep these things at the periphery of the poem? Why do you not move them to the center, where they belong?

But the woman who looks back at me is uncomprehending. If she answers at all, it will be with the rhetoric of a callow apprenticeship: that the poem is pure process, that the technical encounter is the one which guarantees all others. She will speak about the dissonance of the line and the necessity for the stanza. And so on. And so on.

"For what is the poet responsible?" asks Allen Tate. "He is responsible for the virtue proper to him as a poet, for his special *arete*: for the mastery of a disciplined language which will not shun the full report of the reality conveyed to him by his awareness."

She is a long way, that young woman—with her gleaming cup and her movement jargon—from the full report of anything. In her lack of any sense of implication or complication, she might as well be a scientist in the thirties, bombarding uranium with neutrons.

If I try now to analyze why such a dialogue would be a waste of time, I come up with several reasons. One of them is that it would take years for me to see, let alone comprehend, certain realities. Not until the oilskin tablecloth was well folded and the sprawling town had become a rapacious city, and the attic flat was a house in the suburbs, could I accept the fact that I was a woman and a poet in a culture which had the greatest difficulty associating the two ideas. "A woman must often take a critical stance towards her social, historical and cultural position in order to experience her own quest," writes the American poet and feminist Rachel Blau de Plessis. "Poems of the self's growth, or of self-knowledge may often include or be preceded by a questioning of major social prescriptions about the shape women's experience should take." In years to come I would never be sure whether my poems had generated the questions or the questions had facilitated the poems. All that lay ahead. "No poet," says Eliot, "no artist of any kind, has his complete meaning alone." In the meantime, I existed whether I liked it or not in a mesh, a web, a labyrinth of associations. Of poems past and present. Contemporary poems. Irish poems.

v.

Irish poetry was predominantly male. Here or there you found a small eloquence, like "After Aughrim" by Emily Lawless. Now and again, in discussion, you heard a woman's name. But the lived vocation, the craft witnessed by a human life—that was missing. And I missed it. Not in the beginning, perhaps. But later, when perceptions of womanhood began to redirect my own work, what I regretted was the absence of an expressed poetic life which would have dignified and revealed mine. The influence of absences should not be underestimated. Isolation itself can have a powerful effect in the life of a young writer. "I'm talking about real influence now," says Raymond Carver. "I'm talking about the moon and the tide."

I turned to the work of Irish male poets. After all, I thought of myself as an Irish poet. I wanted to locate myself within the Irish poetic tradition. The dangers and stresses in my own themes gave me an added incentive to discover a context for them. But what I found dismayed me.

The majority of Irish male poets depended on women as motifs in their poetry. They moved easily, deftly, as if by right among images of women in which I did not believe and of which I could not approve. The women in their poems were often passive, decorative, raised to emblematic status. This was especially true where the woman and the idea of the nation were mixed: where the nation became a woman and the woman took on a national posture.

The trouble was these images did good service as ornaments. In fact, they had a wide acceptance as ornaments by readers of Irish poetry. Women in such poems were frequently referred to approvingly as mythic, emblematic. But to me these passive and simplified women seemed a corruption. Moreover, the transaction they urged on the reader, to accept them as mere decoration, seemed to compound the corruption. For they were not decorations, they were not ornaments. However distorted these images, they had their roots in a suffered truth.

What had happened? How had the women of our past—the women of a long struggle and a terrible survival—undergone such a transformation? How had they suffered Irish history and rooted themselves in the speech and memory of the Achill woman, only to reemerge in Irish poetry as fictive queens and national sibyls?

The more I thought about it, the more uneasy I became. The wrath and grief of Irish history seemed to me, as it did to many, one of our true possessions. Women were part of that wrath, had endured that grief. It seemed to me a species of human insult that at the end of all, in certain Irish poems, they should become elements of style rather than aspects of truth.

The association of the feminine and the national—and the consequent simplification of both—are not, of course, a monopoly of Irish poetry. "All my life," writes Charles de

Gaulle, "I have thought about France in a certain way. The emotional side of me tends to imagine France like the princess in the fairy tale, or the Madonna of the Frescoes." De Gaulle's words point up the power of nationhood to edit the reality of womanhood. Once the idea of a nation influences the perception of a woman, then that woman is suddenly and inevitably simplified. She can no longer have complex feelings and aspirations. She becomes the passive projection of a national idea.

Irish poems simplified women most at the point of intersection between womanhood and Irishness. The further the Irish poem drew away from the idea of Ireland, the more real and persuasive became the images of women. Once the pendulum swung back, the simplifications started again. The idea of the defeated nation's being reborn as a triumphant woman was central to a certain kind of Irish poem. Dark Rosaleen. Cathleen ni Houlihan. The nation as woman; the woman as national muse.

The more I looked at it, the more it seemed to me that in relation to the idea of a nation many, if not most, Irish male poets had taken the soft option. The irony was that few Irish poets were nationalists. By and large, they had eschewed the fervor and crudity of that ideal. But long after they had rejected the politics of Irish nationalism, they continued to deploy the emblems and enchantments of its culture. It was the culture, not the politics, which informed Irish poetry: not the harsh awakenings but the old dreams.

In all of this I did not blame nationalism. Nationalism

seemed to me inevitable in the Irish context, a necessary hallucination within Joyce's nightmare of history. I did blame Irish poets. Long after it was necessary, Irish poetry had continued to trade in the exhausted fictions of the nation, had allowed those fictions to edit ideas of womanhood and modes of remembrance. Some of the poetry produced by such simplifications was, of course, difficult to argue with. It was difficult to deny that something was gained by poems which used the imagery and emblem of the national muse. Something was gained, certainly, but only at an aesthetic level. While what was lost occurred at the deepest, most ethical level, and what was lost was what I valued. Not just the details of a past. Not just the hungers, the angers. These, however terrible, remain local. But the truth these details witness—human truths of survival and humiliation—these also were suppressed along with the details. Gone was the suggestion of any complicated human suffering. Instead you had the hollow victories, the passive images, the rhyming queens.

I knew that the women of the Irish past were defeated. I knew it instinctively long before the Achill woman pointed down the hill to the Keel shoreline. What I objected to was that Irish poetry should defeat them twice.

"I have not written day after day," says Camus, "because I desire the world to be covered with Greek statues and masterpieces. The man who has such a desire does exist in me. But I have written so much because I cannot keep from being drawn toward everyday life, toward those, whoever they may be, who are humiliated. They need to hope and, if all keep silent, they will be forever deprived of hope and we with them."

This argument originates in some part from my own need to locate myself in a powerful literary tradition in which until then, or so it seemed to me, I had been an element of design rather than an agent of change. But even as a young poet, and certainly by the time my work confronted me with some of these questions, I had already had a vivid, human witness of the stresses which a national literature can impose on a poet. I had already seen the damage it could do.

VI.

I remember the Dublin of the sixties almost more vividly than the city which usurped it. I remember its grace and emptiness and the old hotels with their chintzes and Sheffield trays. In one of these I had tea with Padraic Colum. I find it hard to be exact about the year, somewhere around the middle sixties. But I have no difficulty at all about the season. It was winter. We sat on a sofa by the window overlooking the street. The lamps were on, and a fine rain was being glamorized as it fell past their cowls.

Colum was then in his eighties. He had come from his native Longford in the early years of the century to a Dublin fermenting with political and literary change. Yeats admired his 1907 volume of poetry, *Wild Earth*. He felt the Ireland Colum proposed fitted neatly into his own ideas. "It is un-beautiful Ireland," Yeats writes, "he will contrast finely with our Western dialect-makers."

In old photographs Colum looks the part: curly-headed, dark, winsome. In every way he was a godsend to the Irish Revival. Nobody would actually have used the term *peasant poet*. But then nobody would have needed to. Such things were understood.

The devil, they say, casts no shadow. But that folk image applies to more than evil. There are writers in every country who begin in the morning of promise but by the evening, mysteriously, have cast no shadow and left no mark. Colum is one of them. For some reason, although he was eminently placed to deal with the energies of his own culture, he failed to do so. His musical, tender, hopeful imagination glanced off the barbaric griefs of the nineteenth century. It is no good fudging the issue. Very few of his poems now look persuasive on the page. All that heritage which should have been his— rage robbed of language, suffering denied its dignity—some- how eluded him. When he met it at all, it was with a borrowed sophistication.

Now in old age he struggled for a living. He transited stoically between Dublin and New York, giving readings, writing articles. He remained open and approachable. No doubt for this reason, I asked him what he really thought of Yeats. He paused for a moment. His voice had a distinctive, treble resonance. When he answered, it was high and em- phatic. "Yeats hurt me," he said. "He expected too much of me."

I have never been quite sure what Colum meant. What I understand by his words may be different from their intent.

But I see his relation with the Irish Revival as governed by corrupt laws of supply and demand. He could be tolerated only if he read the signals right and acquiesced in his role as a peasant poet. He did not, and he could not. To be an accomplice in such a distortion required a calculation he never possessed. But the fact that he was screen-tested for it suggests how relentless the idea of Irishness in Irish poetry has been.

Colum exemplified something else to me. Here also was a poet who had been asked to make the journey, in one working lifetime, from being the object of Irish poems to being their author. He too, as an image, had been unacceptably simplified in all those poems about the land and the tenantry. So that—if he was to realize his identity—not only must he move from image to image maker, he must also undo the simplifications of the first by his force and command of the second. I suspect he found the imaginative stresses of that transit beyond his comprehension, let alone his strength. And so something terrible happened to him. He wrote Irish poetry as if he were still the object of it. He wrote with the passivity and simplification of his own reflection looking back at him from poems, plays and novels in which the so-called Irish peasant was a son of the earth, a cipher of the national cause. He had the worst of both worlds.

VII.

Like Colum, Francis Ledwidge was born at the sharp end of history. He was an Irish poet who fought as a British soldier, a writer in a radical situation who used a conservative idiom to support it, and Ledwidge's short life was full of contradiction. He was in his early twenties when he died in the First World War.

Despite his own marginal and pressured position, Ledwidge used the conventional language of romantic nationalism. Not always; perhaps not often. But his poem on the death of the leaders of the Easter Rising, "The Blackbirds," is a case in point. It is, in a small way, a celebrated poem, and I have certainly not chosen it because it represents careless or shoddy work. Far from it. It is a skillful poem, adroit and quick in its rhythms, with an underlying sweetness of tone. For all that, it provides an example of a gifted poet who did not resist the contemporary orthodoxy. Perhaps he might have had he lived longer and learned more. As it was, Ledwidge surrendered easily to the idioms of the Irish Revival. This in turn meant that he could avail himself of a number of approved stereotypes and, chief among them, the easy blend of feminine and national. Even here he could exercise a choice although, it must be said, a limited one. He could have had the Young Queen or the Old Mother. As it happens, he chose the Poor Old Woman. But we are in no doubt what he means:

THE BLACKBIRDS

I heard the Poor Old Woman say
"At break of day the fowler came,
And took my blackbirds from their songs
Who loved me well thro' shame and blame.

141

"No more from lovely distances
Their songs shall bless me mile from mile,
Nor to white Ashbourne call me down
To wear my crown another while.

"With bended flowers the angels mark
For the skylark the place they lie.
From there its little family
Shall dip their wings first in the sky.

"And when the first surprise of flight
Sweet songs excite, from the far dawn
Shall there come blackbirds, loud with love,
Sweet echoes of the singers gone.

"But in the lonely hush of eve
Weeping I grieve the silent bills"
I heard the Poor Old Woman say
In Derry of the little hills.

I am not sure this poem would pass muster now. There
are too many sugary phrases—"loud with love" and "shame
and blame"—evoking the very worst of Georgian poetry. But
Ledwidge was young, and the impulse for the poem was historical. The 1916 leaders were dead. He was at a foreign front.
The poem takes on an extra resonance if it is read as a concealed elegy for his own loyalties.

What is more interesting is how, in his attempt to make
the feminine stand in for the national, he has simplified the

woman in the poem almost out of existence. She is in no sense the poor old woman of the colloquial expression. There are no vulnerabilities here, no human complexities. She is a Poor Old Woman in capital letters. A mouthpiece. A sign.

Therefore, the poem divides into two parts: one vital, one inert. The subject of the poem appears to be the woman. But appearances deceive. She is merely the object, the pretext. The real subject is the blackbirds. They are the animated substance of the piece. They call from "lovely distances"; their "sweet songs" "excite" and "bless." Whatever imaginative power the lyric has, it comes from these birds. Like all effective images, the blackbirds have a life outside the poem. They take their literal shape from the birds we know, and to these they return an emblematic force. They continue to be vital once the poem is over.

The woman, on the other hand, is a diagram. By the time the poem is over, she has become a dehumanized ornament. When her speaking part finishes, she goes out of the piece and out of our memory. At best she has been the engine of the action, a convenient frame for the proposition.

The question worth asking is whether this fusion of national and feminine, this interpretation of one by the other are inevitable. It was after all common practice in Irish poetry: Mangan's "Dark Rosaleen" comes immediately to mind. In fact, the custom and the practice reached back, past the songs and simplifications of the nineteenth century, into the bardic tradition itself. Daniel Corkery refers to this in his analysis of the Aisling convention in *The Hidden Ireland*. "The vision the poet sees," he writes there, "is always the spirit of Ireland as a majestic and radiant maiden."

So many male Irish poets—the later Yeats seems to me a rare exception—have feminized the national and nationalized the feminine that from time to time it has seemed there is no other option. But an Irish writer who turned away from such usages suggests that there was, in fact, another and more subversive choice.

In the opening pages of *Ulysses* Joyce describes an old woman. She climbs the steps to the Martello tower, darkening its doorway. She is, in fact, the daily milkwoman. But no sooner has she started to pour a quart of milk into Stephen's measure than she begins to shimmer and dissolve into legendary images: "Silk of the kine and poor old woman, names given her in old times. A wandering crone, lowly form of an immortal serving her conqueror and her gay betrayer, their common cuckquean, a messenger from the secret morning. To serve or to upbraid, whether he could not tell: but scorned to beg her favour."

The same phrase as Ledwidge uses—poor old woman—is included here. But whereas Ledwidge uses it with a straight face, Joyce dazzles it with irony. By reference and inference, he shows himself to be intent on breaking the traditional association of Ireland with ideas of womanhood and tragic motherhood. After all, these simplifications are part and parcel of what he, Joyce, has painfully rejected. They are some of the reason he is in exile from the mythos of his own country.

144

Now by cunning inflations, by disproportions of language, he takes his revenge. He holds at a glittering, manageable distance a whole tendency in national thought and expression; and dismisses it. But then Joyce is a poetic moralist. Much of *Ulysses,* after all, is invested in Dedalus's search for the ethical shadow of his own aesthetic longings. He has a difficult journey ahead of him. And Joyce has no intention of letting him be waylaid, so early in the book, by the very self-deceptions he has created him to resolve.

VIII.

It is easy, and intellectually seductive, for a woman artist to walk away from the idea of a nation. There has been, and there must continue to be, a great deal of debate about the energies and myths women writers should bring with them into a new age. "Start again" has been the cry of some of the best feminist poets. "Wipe clean the slate, start afresh." It is a cry with force and justice behind it. And it is a potent idea: to begin in a new world, clearing the desert as it were, making it blossom, even making the rain.

In any new dispensation the idea of a nation must seem an expendable construct. After all, it has never admitted women. Its flags and songs and battle cries, even its poetry, as I've suggested, make use of feminine imagery. But that is all. The true voice and vision of women are routinely excluded.

Then why did I not walk away? Simply because I was not free to. For all my quarrels with the concept, and no doubt partly because of them, I needed to find and repossess that idea at some level of repose. Like the swimmer in Adrienne Rich's poem "Diving into the Wreck," I needed to find out "the damage that was done and the treasures that prevail." I knew the idea was flawed. But if it was flawed, it was also one of the vital human constructs of a place in which, like Leopold Bloom, I was born. More important, as a friend and feminist scholar said to me, we ourselves are constructed by the construct. I might be the author of my poems; I was not the author of my past. However crude the diagram, the idea of a nation remained the rough graphic of an ordeal. In some subterranean way I felt myself to be part of that ordeal; its fragmentations extended into mine.

"I am an invisible man . . ." begins the Prologue of Ralph Ellison's *Invisible Man*. "I am invisible, understand, simply because people refuse to see me. Like the bodiless heads you see sometimes in circus sideshows, it is as though I have been surrounded by mirrors of hard, distorting glass. When they approach me they see only my surroundings, themselves, or figments of their imagination—indeed, everything and anything except me."

In an important sense, Ellison's words applied to the sort of Irish poem which availed of that old, potent blurring of feminine and national. In such poems not only was the real woman behind the image not explored, she was never even seen. It was a subtle mechanism, subtle and corrupt. And it was linked, I believed, to a wider sequence of things not seen.

A society, a nation, a literary heritage are always in danger of making up their communicable heritage from their visible elements. Women, as it happens, are not especially visible in Ireland. This came to me early and with personal force. I realized when I published a poem that what was seen of me, what drew approval, if it was forthcoming at all, was the poet. The woman, by and large, was invisible. It was an unsettling discovery. Yet I came to believe that my invisibility as a woman was a disguised grace. It had the power to draw me, I sensed, towards realities like the Achill woman. It made clear to me that what she and I shared, apart from those fragile moments of talk, was the danger of being edited out of our own literature by conventional tribalisms.

Marginality within a tradition, however painful, confers certain advantages. It allows the writer clear eyes and a quick critical sense. Above all, the years of marginality suggest to such a writer—and I am speaking of myself now—the real potential of subversion. I wanted to relocate myself within the Irish poetic tradition. I felt the need to do so. I thought of myself as an Irish poet, although I was fairly sure it was not a category that readily suggested itself in connection with my work. A woman poet is rarely regarded as an automatic part of a national poetic tradition, and for the reasons I have already stated. She is too deeply woven into the passive texture of that tradition, too intimate a part of its imagery, to be allowed her freedom. She may know, as an artist, that she is now the maker of the poems and not merely the subject of them. The critique is slow to catch up. There has been a growing tendency in the last few years for academics and critics in this country to discuss women's poetry as a subculture, to keep it quarantined from the main body of poetry. I thought it vital that women poets such as myself should establish a discourse with the idea of the nation. I felt sure that the most effective way to do this was by subverting the previous terms of that discourse. Rather than accept the nation as it appeared in Irish poetry, with its queens and muses, I felt the time had come to rework those images by exploring the emblematic relation between my own feminine experience and a national past.

The truths of womanhood and the defeats of a nation? An improbable intersection? At first sight perhaps. Yet the idea of it opened doors in my mind which had hitherto been closed fast. I began to think there was indeed a connection, that my womanhood and my nationhood were meshed and linked at some root. It was not just that I had a womanly feeling for those women who waited with handcarts, went into the sour stomach of ships and even—according to terrible legend—eyed their baby's haunches speculatively in the hungers of the 1840s. It was more than that. I was excited by the idea that if there really was an emblematic relation between the defeats of womanhood and the suffering of a nation, I need only prove the first in order to reveal the second. If so, then Irishness and womanhood, those tormenting fragments of my youth, could at last stand in for each other. Out of a painful apprenticeship and an ethical dusk, the laws of metaphor beckoned me.

I was not alone. "Where women write strongly as women," says Alicia Ostriker, the American poet and critic, in her book *Stealing the Language,* "it is clear their intention is to subvert the life and literature they inherit." This was not only true of contemporary women poets. In the terrible years between 1935 and 1940 the Russian poet Anna Akhmatova composed "Requiem." It was written for her only son, Lev Gumilev, who at the start of the Stalinist terror had been arrested, released, rearrested. Then, like so many others, he disappeared into the silence of a Leningrad prison. For days, months, years Akhmatova queued outside. The "Epilogue to the Requiem" refers to that experience. What is compelling and instructive is the connection it makes between her womanhood and her sense of a nation as a community of grief. The country she wishes to belong to, to be commemorated by is the one revealed to her by her suffering.

And if ever in this country they should want
To build me a monument

I consent to that honour
But only on condition that they

Erect it not on the sea-shore where I was born:
My last links with that were broken long ago,

Nor by the stump in the Royal Gardens
Where an inconsolable young shade is seeking me

But here, where I stood for three hundred hours
And where they never, never opened the doors for me

Lest in blessed death I should ever forget
The grinding scream of the Black Marias,

The hideous clanging gate, the old
Woman wailing like a wounded beast.

(Translation D. M. Thomas)

IX.

I want to summarize this argument. At the same time I
am concerned that in the process it may take on a false symmetry. I have, after all, been describing ideas and impressions
as if they were events. I have been proposing thoughts and
perceptions in a way they did not and could not occur. I have
given hard shapes and definite outlines to feelings which were
far more hesitant.

The reality was different. Exact definitions do not happen in the real life of a poet, and certainly not in mine. I have
written here about the need to repossess the idea of a nation.
But there was nothing assured or automatic about it. "It is not
in the darkness of belief that I desire you," says Richard
Rowan at the end of Joyce's *Exiles,* "but in restless, living,
wounding doubt." I had the additional doubts of a writer
who knows that a great deal of her literary tradition has been
made up in ignorance of her very existence, that its momen-
tum has been predicated on simplifications of its complexity.
Yet I still wished to enter that tradition, although I knew my
angle of entry must be oblique. None of it was easy. I reached
tentative havens after figurative storms. I came to understand
what Mallarmé meant when he wrote: "Each newly acquired
truth was born only at the expense of an impression that

flamed up and then burned itself out, so that its particular darkness could be isolated."

My particular darkness as an Irish poet has been the subject of this piece. But there were checks and balances. I was, as I have said, a woman in a literary tradition which simplified them. I was also a poet lacking the precedent and example of previous Irish women poets. These were the givens of my working life. But if these circumstances displaced my sense of relation to the Irish past in Irish poetry, they also forced me into a perception of the advantages of being able to move, with almost surreal inevitability, from being within the poem to being its maker. A hundred years ago I might have been a motif in a poem. Now I could have a complex self within my own poem. Part of that process entailed being a privileged witness to forces of reaction in Irish poetry.

Some of these I have named. The tendency to fuse the national and the feminine, to make the image of the woman the pretext of a romantic nationalism—these have been weaknesses in Irish poetry. These simplifications isolated and estranged me as a young poet. They also made it clearer to me that my own discourse must be subversive. In other words, that I must be vigilant to write of my own womanhood— whether it was revealed to me in the shape of a child or a woman from Achill—in such a way that I never colluded with the simplified images of women in Irish poetry.

When I was young, all this was comfortless. I took to heart the responsibility of making my own critique, even if for years it consisted of little more than accusing Irish poetry in my own mind of deficient ethics. Even now I make no apology for such a critique. I believe it is still necessary. Those simplified women, those conventional reflexes and reflexive feminizations of the national experience, those static, passive, ornamental figures do not credit to a poetic tradition which has been, in other respects, radical and innovative, capable of both latitude and compassion.

But there is more to it. As a young poet I would not have felt so threatened and estranged if the issue had merely been the demands a national program makes on a country's poetry. The real issue went deeper. When I read those simplifications of women, I felt there was an underlying fault in Irish poetry, almost a geological weakness. All good poetry depends on an ethical relation between imagination and image. Images are not ornaments; they are truths. When I read about Cathleen ni Houlihan or the Old Woman of the Roads or Dark Rosaleen, I felt that a necessary ethical relation was in danger of being violated over and over again, that a merely ornamental relation between imagination and image was being handed on from poet to poet, from generation to generation, was becoming orthodox poetic practice. It was the violation, even more than the simplification, which alienated me.

No poetic imagination can afford to regard an image as a temporary aesthetic maneuver. Once the image is distorted, the truth is demeaned. That was the heart of it all as far as I was concerned. In availing themselves of the old convention, in using and reusing women as icons and figments, Irish poets were not just dealing with emblems. They were also evading the real women of an actual past, women whose silence their poetry should have broken. In so doing, they ran the risk of turning a terrible witness into an empty decoration.

Writers, if they are wise, do not make their home in any comfort within a national tradition. However vigilant the writer, however enlightened the climate, the dangers persist. So too do the obligations. There is a recurring temptation for any nation, and for any writer who operates within its field of force, to make an ornament of the past, to turn the losses to victories and to restate humiliations as triumphs. In every age language holds out narcosis and amnesia for this purpose. But such triumphs in the end are unsustaining and may, in fact, be corrupt.

If a poet does not tell the truth about time, his or her work will not survive it. Past or present, there is a human dimension to time, human voices within it and human griefs ordained by it. Our present will become the past of other men and women. We depend on them to remember it with the complexity with which it was suffered. As others, once, depended on us.

7.

THE WOMAN THE PLACE THE POET

There is a duality to place. There is the place which existed before you and will continue after you have gone. For the purposes of this argument there are two. First of all, Dundrum, a Dublin suburb: I have lived here for twenty-three of my forty-nine years, longer, in fact, than in any other single environment. The second—an altogether darker, grimmer region—is a hundred miles southwest. Both of them prove to me there is the place that happened and the place that happens to you. That there are moments—in work, in perception, in experience—when they are hard to disentangle from each other. And that, at such times, the inward adventure can become so enmeshed with the outward continuum that we live, not in one or the other, but at the point of intersection.

I suspect this account is about just such an intersection. It is, of course, a particular version of particular locales. But there may well be a more general truth disguised in it: that what we call place is really only that detail of it which we understand to be ourselves. "That's my Middle West," writes Fitzgerald in *The Great Gatsby,* "not the wheat or the prairies or the lost Swede towns but the thrilling returning trains of my youth and the streetlamps and sleigh bells in the frosty dark and the shadows of holly wreaths thrown by lighted windows on the snow. I am part of that."

Questions of place were far from my mind that first winter, the second of our marriage, when we moved out here. We unpacked our books, put up our shelves and looked doubtfully at the raw floors and white walls of a new house. From the upstairs window we saw little to console us. Dundrum at this time, in the early seventies, was already starting to wander out towards the foothills of the Dublin mountains. On those winter nights, in the first weeks of January, we learned to look for the lamps on the hills after dark, yellow and welcome as nocturnal crocuses.

For all that, we were disoriented. I, at least, was thoroughly urban. The Dublin I had known until then was a sympathetic prospect of stone and water and wet dusks over

Stephen's Green, a convivial town of coffee and endlessly re-
newable talk. I knew nothing of the city of contingencies.
Now here it was, visible and oppressive and still at a distance
from the love I would come to feel for it.

The road outside our window was only half laid. The
house next door was built, and the houses opposite were finished. There was good progress about halfway down our
road.

Walls were up; roofs were on; gardens were rotovated
and, in some cases, even seeded. After about seven houses,
however, the prospect gave out into mud and rubble. In a
cold dusk it all seemed incomplete and improbable.

Now, on a summer morning, when the whitebeams are
so thick they almost obscure the mimicking greens and grays
of the mountains, I look back to that time and consider its
revelations. That first spring, however, I thought of little else
but practicalities. Ovens and telephones became images and
emblems of the real world. The house was cold. We had no
curtains. At night the lights on the hills furnished the upper
rooms with a motif of adventure and estrangement. In the
morning the hills marched in, close or distant, promising rain
or the dry breezes of a March day.

Now, also, I find myself wishing I had had less of a sense
of locale and more of local history. It was all too easy to allow
a day to come down to the detail of a fabric or the weight of
a chicken. If I had looked about me with a wider sense of
curiosity, I would have noticed more. To start with, I would

have seen a past as well as a present. I was oblivious, for instance, of the fact that Dundrum had its roots in Anglo-Norman times, when the castle had first been built to ward off the Wicklow clans. Its destiny as a residential center had been settled centuries later, when the Harcourt Street railway line was opened. With its assistance, the distance between Dundrum and the city center became a mere sixteen minutes.

It was all changing by the time we arrived. Indeed, the arrival of young couples like ourselves was a signal of that change. But enough distinction remained to give a sense of the grace and equilibrium of the place it had been. Granted, the farriers at the corner of the village had been gone some twenty years. But the cobbler remained. Further down, the experiment of a mink farm had failed and a shopping center was in the process of replacing it. Above all, the location remained: the wonderful poise of the village at the edge of theatrical, wooded cliffs and under the incline of the Dublin mountains.

Occasionally I would be aware of the contradictions and poignance of our new home. But in the main I missed the fact that the shops, the increasing traffic, the lights on the hills and we ourselves were not isolated pieces of information.

They and we were part of a pattern, one that was being repeated throughout Ireland in those years. Before our eyes, and because of them, a village was turning into a suburb.

♦ ♦ ♦

My account of the other place begins with a journey. If this were a poem, that journey would become a descent. I packed the car one summer night—a camera, biscuits—and set out at dawn. I left the suburb folded in light, the white-beams already taking on a grayish glitter, a dog barking somewhere.

I drove southwest. The Irish roads offer no ornament. Fifty years ago all but the most direct of them would have been witnessed only by locals going at the pace of the herd. The average road between small towns is bordered by fern-choked ditches and, in summer, by weedy altitudes of cow parsley.

It was summer now. And now, for a brief moment, those roadsides were colored. I was used to blond splashes of coltsfoot and, further west, to the pageant of hawthorn. What kept taking my eye was something different: a shrubby, low plant with blue flowers. It was unsettling. I had seen that shade of blue before in the lips of old people—the terrible blush of shallow breathing. Now it occurred at every turn; it became the color of the journey. Later I would find out that the name of the plant was cyanotis.

By midmorning I was turning left at the rock of Cashel, the old stone fort of the kings of Munster. Its towers and sharp rock facings still look out over the fertile plain of Tipperary. Ten miles up the road and I had reached Clonmel. I asked an elderly man for directions. He pointed me to the Old Western Road on the far side of the town. Then he lifted his hand higher to the peak of the Comeragh Mountains, which reared up at the end of the street. You could get a grouse up there, he assured me.

♦ ♦ ♦

I had lived in cities all my life. I made a distinction between a city you loved and a city you submitted to. I had not loved London, for instance, where I had spent the greater part of my childhood. The iron and gutted stone of its postwar prospect had seemed to me merely hostile. I was not won over by its parks or the scarlet truculence of its buses, which carried me forwards and backwards from school. Those were the early fifties. I learned quickly, by inference at school and reference at home, that the Irish were unwelcome in London.

I absorbed enough of that information to regard everything, even the jittery gleam from the breastplates of the Horse Guards as they rode through the city, with a sort of churlish inattention. All I knew, all I needed to know, was that none of this was mine.

New York was a different matter. The noise and speed of it persuaded me to try again. I was just twelve when I went there. I liked putting on skates in summer and shorts in winter. I had never known extremes, whether of dress or season, before, and on the edge of puberty, I responded to their drama.

Then there was Dublin. By the time I came to know it, those other cities had prepared me to relish a place which had something of the theater of a city and all of the intimacy of a town. These were the early sixties. There were still coffee bars set into the basements of Georgian houses, where a turf fire burned from four o'clock in the afternoon and you could get brown scones with your coffee.

None of it prepared me for a suburb. There is, after all, a necessity about cities. By the time you come to them, there is something finished and inevitable about their architecture, even about their grime. You accept both.

A suburb is altogether more fragile and transitory. To start with, it is composed of lives in a state of process. The public calendar defines a city; banks are shut and shops are opened. But the private one shapes a suburb. It waxes and wanes on christenings, weddings, birthdays. In one year it can seem a whole road is full of bicycles, roller skates, jumble sales. Garages will be wide open, with children selling comics and stale raisin buns. There will be shouting and calling far into the summer night. Almost as soon, it seems, the same road will be quiet. The bicycles will be gone. The shouting and laughing will be replaced by one or two dogs barking in back gardens. Curtains will be drawn till late morning, and doors will stay closed.

◆ ◆ ◆

Clonmel is the county town of Tipperary. Its name comes from the Irish, *cluain meala*—meadow of honey. This is a storied part of Ireland. The Danes visited it in the eighth century. Cromwell fixed his batteries here on rising ground to the north of the town and received one of the worst reverses of his Irish campaign.

In the first decades of the nineteenth century Clonmel prospered. Travelers praised its regular streets, its well-built houses, "the greater part of which are rough cast, and are either cream-coloured or white, save here and there one of neat appearance, whose front is often curiously ornamented with blue slates." The rows of thatched cabins had been cleared from the outskirts of the town. Corn stores were hoarded by the river; the quays were embanked with limestone ashlar. "Mr. Banfield," simpers one contemporary account, "has added much to the appearance of the town by the erection of a row of very genteel houses."

It was a garrison town. Two militia regiments of the Tipperary Artillery were quartered there. Sometime after the Crimean War my great-great-grandfather took up a position on this headquarters staff as a sergeant major. He could read and write, that much is certain. Otherwise he could not have kept accounts or made a note of provisions. And he was something of a dandy. "He had a head of thick nut-brown hair the colour of your own," wrote my grandfather to his son. "My mother used to tell us how, on parade days when his toilet was of special care, he used to curse the waves in his hair that prevented him getting it to lie as he wanted."

A peacock. A soldier. A literate Irishman in a dark century. But I had not come to find him. I turned out past the town center and took the Old Western Road. After a hundred yards or so it takes a broad, bluish turn—those shrubs again—and becomes a gradual hill. To the right there is a sudden crest with a straggle of buildings.

I walked up the hill. It was steep, the path winding and edged by trees. They had a dark, inappropriate presence. I would not have recognized cypress or yew, but these I thought deserved their legend. The higher I went, the more the valley—the old meadow of honey—scrolled beneath me.

The buildings were grim. One ran the length of the hill, an institutional ramble of granite and drainpipes. Below it, further down, was a smaller building. Over to one side were a separate house and, further down again, at road level, a small church and a deserted school.

I needed to see all this. Sometime in 1874, with a growing family to maintain, my great-grandfather cast around for a secure position. He took the only one vacant—"the only one," as my grandfather put it, "to which a Catholic could hope for appointment." Sometime in the autumn of that year, with the approval of the Board of Guardians, he became the master of that most dreaded Irish institution the workhouse.

Now, more than a hundred years later, it was hard enough to distinguish from that scatter of granite which building was which. The largest one now served as the local hospital. I went inside. Two women, one elderly, both dressed as nurses, came over. The older one was sweet-faced and vague. The younger one was definite. Yes, this had been the poorhouse—she gave it its folk name—this building overlooking the hill.

I came out into sunshine. Poetic license is an age-old concept. Traditionally poets have been free to invoke place as a territory between invention and creation. I myself might once have proposed it as an act of imagination or an article of faith. But here, on a blue summer morning, I could feel it to be what it has been for so many: brute, choiceless fact.

♦ ♦ ♦

We yield to our present, but we choose our past. In a defeated country like Ireland we choose it over and over again, relentlessly, obsessively. Standing there looking back at the bleak length of the building, I refused to imagine him— my ancestor, with his shock of nut brown hair. The truth was I was ashamed of his adroit compliance, the skillful opportunism by which he had ensured our family's survival.

Instead I imagined a woman. A woman like myself, with two small children, who must have come to this place as I came to the suburb. She would have come here in her twenties or thirties. But whereas my arrival in the suburb marked a homecoming, hers in the workhouse would have initiated a final and almost certainly fatal homelessness. At an age when I was observing the healings of place, she would have been a scholar of its violations.

There were several reasons why she might have been there. The most obvious, unmarried motherhood, remains the most likely. But she could as easily have been a survivor of an eviction. Hundreds of them—complete with bailiff and battering ram—took place in Ireland every year of that century. British cartoons and a few old photographs tell the story: wretched homemade tables strewn on the road, the cabin door barred, the windows boarded up. She may even have married a soldier. Clonmel, after all, was a garrison town. Two regiments were quartered there. Hadn't my own great-grandfather fallen for the stagy glitter of the uniforms. Didn't his wife fear that her children might do the same?

Whatever her reasons for being there, her sufferings would have been terrible. When I looked up the hill, I could see how the main length of the building ended in a kitchen garden. There was a small house with blunt gables and an outhouse. Was this where my great-grandfather lived? Where he stabled his pony, collected his ration, sheltered his children in the security of his position as overseer of other people's tragedies? At least, by these visible survivals, I could guess at his existence. There was no trace of hers.

The Clonmel workhouse—or, to give it its more respectable title, the Clonmel Union—was founded in 1838. In that year, and against all informed advice, the English Poor Law of 1834 was extended to Ireland. Until then this building had served as a catchall: asylum, orphanage, geriatric ward. *The Survey of Clonmel,* for instance, published in 1813, clothes its account of it in the chilly language of nineteenth-century altruism: "A very extensive House of Industry was finished two years ago in the west end of the town, both at the public expense of the county and by private subscription. It is a common receptable for all descriptions of mals fortunes, serving at the same time as a place of confinement for vagrants and luna-tics, as well as an asylum for the poor and helpless."

In 1838, when the Poor Law was introduced, Ireland

stood at the edge of its greatest ordeal: the famine. In the next few years the workhouses would fill to overflowing with the children of emigrants, the orphans of typhus, the debris of a preventable tragedy.

Most of the buildings which accommodated them were themselves casualties of bad planning and hasty decision making. The walls and ceilings were not plastered. Limestone was burned on the site and then used as a crude whitewash. Maintenance was scanty. Contemporary accounts tell of sparrows nesting in the downpipes and water leaking through the mortar. Subsistence was deliberately harsh. The diet consisted of oatmeal, bread, milk at times, but by no means always or in every workhouse. In many, the children got gruel instead. In the 1860s a radical improvement consisted in putting ox heads in the soup: three ox heads for each hundred inmates. There were small, carefully planned degradations to go with the larger ones. Children, for instance, were refused footwear whatever the weather. The guardians believed it unwise to get them accustomed to shoes.

By the 1870s, when my great-grandfather became master of the Clonmel Union, there were some improvements. But of what interest are historical modifications to the person—to this woman—for whom suffering is fresh, first time, without memory or hope? She would have felt no hope at 6:00 A.M., when she rose; no hope at 9:00 P.M., when she finished a day of carefully planned monotony.

Yet she also would have seen the coming and going of the seasons. She also, like me, must have seen them in her children's faces. The meadow would have glittered beneath her on fine days; on wet ones the Comeraghs would have loomed in heathery colors. She may not, however, have seen them for long. Statistics argue persuasively that more than likely, she would have died—still of childbearing age—in the fever hospital a hundred yards down the hill. Clonmel was low-lying. The river Suir ran behind its streets with an ornamental sluggishness. Drainage was poor. Every few years typhus swept through the town. Its first victims must have been the inmates of the workhouse. It would have been my great-grandfather's decision where to bury them. He would have consulted the Board of Guardians. There were rules for such things.

II.

And where does poetry come in? Here, as in so many other instances, it enters at the point where myth touches history. Let me explain. At one level I could have said that there were summer dusks and clear, vacant winter mornings when I was certain the suburb nurtured my poetry. I might have found it hard to say how or why. In every season the neighborhood gathered around me and filled my immediate distance. At times it could be a shelter; it was never a cloister. Everywhere you looked there were reminders—a child's bicycle thrown sideways on the grass, a single roller skate, a tree in its first April of blossom—that lives were not lived here in any sort of static pageant but that they thrived, waned, changed, began and ended here.

Inevitably this sense of growth could not remain just at the edge of things. Apart from anything else, time was passing. Roads were laid. Houses were finished. The builders moved out. Summers came and went, and trees began to define the road. Garden walls were put up, and soon enough the voices calling over them on long, bright evenings, the bicycle thrown on its side and the single roller skate belonged to my children. Somewhat to my surprise, I had done what most human beings have done. I had found a world, and I had populated it. In so doing, my imagination had been radically stirred and redirected. It was not, of course, a simple process. In poetry, let alone in life, it never is. It would be wrong, even now, to say that my poetry expressed the suburb. The more accurate version is that my poetry allowed me to experience it.

Yet there remained a sense of unease, as if some part of me could not assent to the reassurance of patterning. On bright days, for no apparent reason, my mind would swerve. Then I could sense, below the levels of my own conscious perception, something different, as if I could still remember—indeed had never forgotten—that place is never so powerful as when it is suffered in silence.

◆ ◆ ◆

At what point does an actual, exact landscape—those details which are recurrent and predictable—begin to blur and soften? Sometimes on a summer evening, walking between my house and a neighbor's, past the whitebeam trees and the bicycles left glinting in the dusk, I could imagine that I myself was a surreal and changing outline, that there was something almost profound in these reliable shadows, that such lives as mine and my neighbors' were mythic, not because of their strangeness but because of their powerful ordinariness. When I reached a point in the road where I could see the children at the end of it, milling around and shrieking in the consciousness that they would have to come in soon, I would stand there with my hand held sickle-shaped to my eyes. Almost always I was just trying to remember which cotton T-shirt one child of mine or the other was wearing so I could pick it out in the summer twilight and go and scoop them up and bring them in. But just occasionally, standing there and breathing in the heavy musks of rose beds and buddleias, I would feel an older and less temporary connection to the moment. Then I would feel all the sweet, unliterate melancholy of women who must have stood as I did, throughout continents and centuries, feeling the timelessness of that particular instant and the cruel time underneath its surface. They must have measured their children, as I did, against the seasons and looked at the hedges and rowan trees, their height and the color of their berries, as an index of the coming loss.

Is it true, as Patrick Kavanagh says in his beautiful poem "Epic," that "gods make their own importance"? Is the origin, in other words, so restless in the outcome that the parish, the homestead, the place are powerful sources as well as practical locations? On those summer evenings, if my thoughts had not been full of details and children, I could have wondered where myth begins. Is it in the fears for harvest and the need for rain? Are its roots in the desire to make the strange familiar, to domesticate the thunder and give a shape to the frost? Or does it have, as Kavanagh argues, a more local and ritual source? Is there something about the repeated action—about lifting a child, clearing a dish, watching the seasons return to a tree and depart from a vista—which reveals a deeper meaning to existence and heals some of the worst abrasions of time?

Not suddenly then, but definitely and gradually, a place I lived became a country of the mind. Perhaps anywhere I had grown used to, raised my children in, written my poetry about would have become this. But a suburb by its very nature—by its hand-to-mouth compromises between town and country—was particularly well suited to the transformation. Looking out my window at familiar things, I could realize that there had always been something compromised in my own relation to places. They had never been permanent. Therefore, I had never developed a permanent perception about them.

Now here at last was permanence: An illusory permanence, of course, but enough stability to make me realize that the deepest sustenances are not in the new or surprising. And with that realization came the surrender of any prospect of loving new things, a prospect so vital when I was younger. Instead many of the things I now did—from the casual gesture of looking out a window to the writing of poems—became an act of possessing the old things in a new way. I watched for the return of the magpies every February to their nest in the poplars just beyond my garden. I took an almost concert hall pleasure, in an August twilight, in listening to the sound of my neighbor's garden shears as she cut and pruned and made things ready for another season.

None of this was purely instinctive; none of it involved an intellectual suppression or simplification. I had a clearer and clearer sense, as time went on, of the meaning of all this to me as a poet. I knew what repetitions meant in poetry. I understood those values in language and restraint.

When Coleridge wrote, in the *Biographia Literaria,* of metrical units as "at first the offspring of passion and then the adopted children of power," I felt I understood a concept of linguistic patterning which both lulled the mind and facilitated the meaning. Now here, in front of me every day, were repetitions which had almost exactly the same effect. The crocuses under the rowan tree. The same child wheeled down to the shops at the same time every day. A car that returned home, with the same dinge on its bumper, every night. And the lamps which sprang into symmetries across our hills at dusk in November.

What were all these if not—as language and music in poetry were—a sequence and repetition which allowed the deeper meanings to emerge: a sense of belonging, of sustenance, of a life revealed, and not restrained, by ritual and patterning?

♦ ♦ ♦

Now let me rewrite that scenario. Let me darken the evening and harden the detail. The road is no longer paved; there are no streetlamps. My own outline is no longer surreal. It is the harsh shape of that woman, that client of my ancestor. My lips now are as blue as hers, the shallow blue of those shrubs. I have no house, no room in which I write, no books. My children are not healthy and noisy. They are the fractions of my own grief which cling at my skirt, their expressions scarred with hunger and doubt. Instead of bright cotton and denim—clothes they pick out and array themselves in—they wear fustian and the hated flannel. And they, like me, are ripe for the fevers which come in off the marshes and stagnate in the water of the town.

Of course this is impossible. The most awkward memory is known to be a figment, not a ghost. Yet even as a figment this woman was important. She cast her shadow across the suburb. She made me doubt the pastoral renewals of day-to-day life. And whenever I tried to find the quick meanings of my day in the deeper ones of the past, she interposed a fierce presence in case the transaction should be too comfortable, too lyric.

It would be wrong to say her presence changed my idea of poetry. But it changed my idea of place. Then again, it would also be true to say that my most optimistic view of place had never excluded her. Familiar, compound ghosts such as she—paragons of dispossession—haunt the Irish present. She is a part of all our histories. The cadences I learned to see in that suburb, those melodies of renewal, had their roots in her silence. There is a hard, unglamorous suffering in such a silence. And I imagined it often, imagined the mute hatred with which she must have looked at my great-grandfather as he descended from his trap, unharnessed his pony.

In thinking about her at all, I was exercising a peculiar, perhaps even a dangerous freedom. It is a freedom inherent in the shifting outlines of a defeated history. Such a history is full of silences. Hers is only one of them. And those silences in turn are the quicksand on which any stable or expressive view of place will forever after be built. The more I thought of her, the more it seemed to me that a sense of place can happen at the very borders of myth and history. In the first instance there are the healing repetitions, the technology of propitiation. In the second there is the consciousness of violent and random event. In the zone between them something happens. Ideas of belonging take on the fluidity of sleep. Here are a nose, an eye, a mouth, but they may belong to different people. And here, on the edge of dream, is a place in which I locate myself as a poet: not exactly the suburb, not entirely the hill colored with blue shrubs, but somewhere composed of both.

I could put it another way. A suburb is all about futures. Trees grow; a small car becomes a bigger one to accommodate new arrivals. Then again, there is little enough history, almost no appeal to memory. The children learn the names of the sweetshop and the bike repair shop. They talk about the sixty-foot tree in the grounds of an old castle. The fact that

the castle is a Norman keep and may cover Norman remains
is of no interest.

A workhouse, on the other hand—to adapt Yeats's
phrase—is the fiery shorthand of a history. Fever, eviction,
the statistics of poverty—it infers them all. The immediate
past of a nation sleeps in its cots and eats its coarse rations. But
what a workhouse lacks is a future.

◆ ◆ ◆

What I have tried to write about here is neither meta-
phorical nor emblematic but something which is, in fact, the
common source of both. There is a quality about the minute
changes, the gradations of a hedge, the small growth of a small
boy which makes a potent image out of an ordinary day in a
suburb. Nothing I have described here can catch the simple
force for me of looking out my window on one of those
mornings at the end of winter when a few small burgundy
rags would be on the wild cherry tree but otherwise everything was bare and possessed a muted sort of expectancy. The
hills would have the staring blues which signaled rain. A car
would pass by. A neighbor's dog would bark, then be silent.
Maybe the daffodils which had been closed the week before
would now be open, after an afternoon of that quick, buttery
sunshine which is the best part of an Irish spring.

But all of this constitutes the present tense. And the present tense, surely, is instructed by the past. And perhaps I want
to say that women poets—Akhmatova and Adrienne Rich

come to mind—are witnesses to the fact that myth is instructed by history, although the tradition is full of poets who argue the opposite with force and eloquence. In my case, to paraphrase the myth, I gradually came to know at what price my seasons—my suburb—had been bought. My underworld was a hundred miles southwest. But there, too, the bargains had been harsh, the outcome a terrible compromise. The woman I imagined—if the statistics are anything to go by—must have lost her children in that underworld, just as I came to possess mine through the seasons of my neighborhood. This account has been about how that past, those images, her compromised life came to find me in the midst of my incomparably easier one. And how I wanted to be found.

8.

It was the early seventies, a time of violence in Northern Ireland. Our front room was a rectangle with white walls, hardly any furniture and a small television chanting deaths and statistics at teatime.

It was also our first winter in the suburb. The weather was cold; the road was half finished. Each morning the fields on the Dublin hills appeared as slates of frost. At night the streetlamps were too few. And the road itself ran out in a gloom of icy mud and builders' huts.

One evening, at the time of the news, I came into the front room with a cup of coffee in my hand. I heard something at the front door. I set down the coffee, switched on the light and went to open the door.

A large, dappled head—a surreal dismemberment in the dusk—swayed low on the doorstep, then attached itself back to a clumsy horse and clattered away. I went out and stood under the streetlamp. I saw its hindquarters retreating, smudged by mist and darkness. I watched it disappear around a corner. The lamp above me hissed and flickered and finally came on fully.

There was an explanation. It was almost certainly a travelers' horse with some memory of our road as a traveling site and our gardens as fields where it had grazed only recently. The memory withstood the surprises of its return, but not for long. It came back four or five times. Each time, as it was startled into retreat, its huge hooves did damage. Crocus bulbs were uprooted. Hedge seedlings were dragged up. Grass seeds were churned out of their place.

Some months later I began to write a poem. I called it "The War Horse." Its argument was gathered around the oppositions of force and formality. Of an intrusion of nature— the horse—menacing the decorous reductions of nature which were the gardens. And of the failure of language to describe such violence and resist it.

I wrote the poem slowly, adding each couplet with care. I was twenty-six years of age. At first, when it was finished, I looked at it with pleasure and wonder. It encompassed a real event. It entered a place in my life and moved beyond it. I was young enough in the craft to want nothing more.

Gradually I changed my mind, although I never disowned the poem. In fact, my doubts were less about it than about my own first sense of its completeness. The poem had drawn me easily into the charm and strength of an apparently public stance. It had dramatized for me what I already suspected: that one part of the poem in every generation is ready to be communally written. To put it another way, there is a poem in each time that waits to be set down and is therefore instantly recognizable once it has been. It may contain sentiments of outrage or details of an occasion. It may invite a general reaction to some particular circumstance. It may appeal to anger or invite a common purpose.

It hardly matters. The point is that to write in that cursive and approved script can seem, for the unwary poet, a blessed lifting of the solitude and skepticism of the poet's life. Images are easily set down; a music of argument is suddenly revealed. Then a difficult pursuit becomes a swift movement. And finally the poem takes on a glamour of meaning against a background of public interest.

Historically—in the epic, in the elegy—this has been an enrichment. But in a country like Ireland, with a nationalist tradition, there are real dangers. In my poem the horse, the hills behind it—these were private emblems which almost immediately took on a communal reference against a background of communal suffering. In a time of violence it would be all too easy to write another poem, and another. To make a construct where the difficult "I" of perception became the easier "we" of a subtle claim. Where an unearned power would be allowed by a public engagement.

In such a poem the poet would be the subject. The object might be a horse, a distance, a human suffering. It hardly mattered. The public authorization would give such sanction to the poet that the object would not just be silent. It would be silenced. The subject would be all-powerful.

At that point I saw that in Ireland, with its national tradition, its bardic past, the confusion between the political poem and the public poem was a dangerous and inviting motif. It encouraged the subject of the poem to be a representative and the object to be ornamental. In such a relation, the dangerous and private registers of feeling of the true political poem would be truly lost. At the very moment when they were most needed.

And yet I had come out of the Irish tradition as a poet. I had opened the books, read the poems, believed the rhetoric when I was young. Writing the political poem seemed to me almost a franchise of the Irish poet, an inherited privilege. I would come to see that it was more and less than that, that like other parts of the poet's life, it would involve more of solitary scruple than communal eloquence. And yet one thing remained steady: I continued to believe that a reading of the energy and virtue of any tradition can be made by looking at the political poem in its time. At who writes it and why. At who can speak in the half-light between event and perception without their voices becoming shadows as Aeneas's rivals did in the underworld of the Sixth Book.

In that winter twilight, seeing the large, unruly horse scrape the crocus bulbs up in his hooves, making my own connections between power and order, I had ventured on my first political poem. I had seen my first political image. I had even understood the difficulties of writing it. What I had not realized was that I myself was a politic within the Irish poem: a young woman who had left the assured identity of a city and its poetic customs and who had started on a life which had no place in them. I had seen and weighed and struggled with the meaning of the horse, the dark night, the sounds of death from the television. I had been far less able to evaluate my own hand on a light switch, my own form backlit under a spluttering streetlight against the raw neighborhood of a sub-urb. And yet without one evaluation the other was incom-plete.

I would learn that it was far more difficult to make my-self the political subject of my own poems than to see the metaphoric possibilities in front of me in a suburban dusk. The difficulty was a disguised blessing. It warned me away from facile definitions. The more I looked at the political poem, the more I saw how easy it was to make the claim and miss the connections. And I wanted to find them.

II.

I could start with the spring of 1843. In that season Ireland faced both ways. In one direction was a hopeful past: Daniel O'Connell's populist oratory and the bill of Catholic emancipation. In the other direction lay the future and catastrophe: the coming famine and the failure of the 1848 Rising.

Early in that year a volume of poetry appeared. It was called *The Spirit of the Nation* and was sold as a sixpenny booklet. It consisted of poems published in the *Nation,* a tabloid newspaper which had started up the previous October.

The founders of the *Nation* were a group of young middle-class men—Thomas Davis, Charles Gavan Duffy and John Blake Dillon—who advocated a new style of Irish nationalism. Their rhetoric was often abstract and intellectual, but their methods were populist and journalistic. They advocated the Irish language, a self-reflective literature and a new self-reliance. They became known as Young Ireland—to distinguish them from O'Connell's older strategies—and in some respects they were indeed different. Irish nationalism, since the passing of the Act of Union in 1800, had undertaken some awkward engagements which it needed to rid itself of if it was to become an effective and persuasive politic. Not the least of these was with British drawing rooms. The songs, letters and speeches of Irish patriots of the twenties and thirties—O'Connell was not innocent of this, and neither was Tom Moore—have the occasional look of a souvenir shop.

Wolfhounds, harps and shamrocks appear with suspicious frequency.

The *Nation* turned its back on British drawing rooms and commended the spiritual intactness of the Irish nation through its articles, poems and polemics. Its natural constituency was the engaged and doomed generation of Irish Catholics who had listened to O'Connell and would die by their hundreds and thousands in the famine. The newspaper cost sixpence and sold widely: At the height of its popularity its sales were ten thousand, an enormous figure in the circumstance. It is hard to judge how widely it reached the landless Catholic class. There are stories of its being read out to listeners in the cabins and cottages. According to Gavan Duffy, it outsold the local newspaper in some provincial towns where "it passed from hand to hand till it was worn to fragments." But it also sought out the young Protestant middle class who, since 1800, had held aloof from the Irish cause. "Gentleman," Davis reminded the students of Trinity College, "you have a country."

The poems in the *Nation* were often written by Davis, but they also included work by James Clarence Mangan and other gifted writers. The titles reveal the themes: "Lament for the Death of Owen Roe O'Neill," "Dark Rosaleen," "Nationality," "The West's Asleep." In the main—James Clarence Mangan was a notable exception—they were crude and memorable: a strange mix of florid imagery and martial invective. This stanza from "Nationality" by Davis gives a fair sampling:

A nation's voice, a nation's voice—
It is a solemn thing
It bids the bondage-sick rejoice—
'Tis stronger than a king.
'Tis like the light of many stars,
The sound of many waves;
Which brightly look through prison bars;
And sweetly sound through caves.
Yet is it noblest, godliest known
When righteous triumph swells its tone.

The mixing of the national and the feminine is also a recurrent usage in the rhetoric of the newspaper. As Davis himself said, referring to Ireland in an address to the Historical Society at Trinity College, "I have thought I saw her spirit from her dwelling, her sorrowing place among the tombs, rising, not without melancholy, yet with a purity and brightness beyond other nations." Added to this was the view of the political poem Davis proposed. "National poetry," he wrote, "presents the most dramatic events, the largest characters, the most impressive scenes and the deepest passions in the language most familiar to us. It magnifies and ennobles our hearts, our intellects, our country and our countrymen; binds us to the land by its condensed and gem-like history. It solaces us in travel, fires us in action . . . is the recognized envoy of our minds among all mankind and to all time."

The *Nation* was influential for several reasons. In the poems it chose and published, it paid an obvious homage to the ballads of the street. In giving an intellectual legitimacy to those cadences, the *Nation* drew them into the mainstream of the nationalist enterprise and made a vital and lasting connection in Irish poetry. More important, in its pages the public poem and the political poem were confused at the very moment when the national tradition was making a claim on Irish poetry which would color its themes and purposes for a century.

III.

No life was less public or apparently political than mine when I first became conscious of all this. I lived in a world familiar to many women. I had a husband, young children and a home. I did the same things over and over again. At night I watched water sluice the milk bottles to a bluish gleam before I put them out on the step. By day I went to collect my children under whitebeam trees and in different weathers.

Yet merely by the act of going upstairs in a winter dusk, merely by starting to write a poem at a window that looked out on the Dublin hills, I was entering a place of force. Just by trying to record the life I lived in the poem I wrote, I had become a political poet.

Part of the reason for this was that my material was already politicized. The image of the woman which I was dealing with had already been allotted a place in the Irish poem. But as object, not subject. Therefore, the life I lived was at variance, in the poetic tradition, with the power and activity of the poet's voice. I not only experienced that life but ex-

183

pressed it. I gave it a speaking part in the previous drama of its silence. But I was aware of resistances and difficulties in doing so. In a fine essay called "What Foremothers?" the wonderful Irish-language poet Nuala ni Dhomnaill writes "how the image of woman in the national tradition is a very real dragon that every Irish woman poet has to fight every time she opens her door."

There was an odd isolation about those years, but an impersonal one. What comes back to me now is not the pain but the paradox. One part of the poem I wrote was in light, the other in shadow. As a woman the life I lived—its dailyness, its complexity—had been given a place of passivity and silence in the very tradition that had given me my voice as a poet.

It seemed I had a choice. I could write my life into the Irish poem in the way tradition dictated—as mythic distaff of the national tradition—or I could confront the fact that in order to write the Irish poem, I would have to alter, for myself, the powerful relations between subject and object which were established there. That in turn involved disrupting the other values encoded in those relations: the authority of the poet. Its place in the historic legend. And the allegory of nationhood which had customarily been shadowed and enmeshed in the image of the woman.

But in reality I had no choice. I was that image come to life. I had walked out of the pages of the *Nation,* the cadences of protest, the regret of emigrant ballads. And yet I spoke with the ordinary and fractured speech of a woman living in a

Dublin suburb, whose claims to the visionary experience would be sooner made on behalf of a child or a tree than a century of struggle. I was a long way from what Davis thought of as a national poet. And yet my relation to the national poem—as its object, its past—was integral and forceful and ominous.

In that was the clue. It seemed to me that the connection between my life and that poem, while private and obsessive, was simultaneously political. Even in the fastness of the suburb I saw the intensity of witness which the previous silent object of a poetic tradition could give as its articulate present.

The more I thought of it, the more it seemed to me that in Ireland the political poem and the public poem should not always be one and the same. On the contrary, given the force of the national tradition and the claim it had made on Irish literature, the political poem stood in urgent need of a subversive private experience to lend it true perspective and authority. An authority which, in my view, could be guaranteed only by an identity—and this included a sexual identity—which the poetic tradition, and the structure of the Irish poem, had almost stifled.

IV.

I do not believe the political poem can be written with truth and effect unless the self who writes that poem—a self in which sexuality must be a factor—is seen to be in a radical relation to the ratio of power to powerlessness with which the political poem is so concerned. This relation, and the way it is construed, are now visibly altered in the Irish poem. One of the characteristics of the political poem—the accruing of power by the speaker in the poem in the face of a perceived powerlessness outside it—has been subverted. At a downright and sensible level, the sense of power a woman speaker might have in an Irish poem today will not just be political; it must also be politicized. In other words, her sense of power inside the poem must be flawed and tempered not just by a perception of powerlessness outside it but also by the memory of her traditional and objectified silence within it.

The final effect of the political poem depends on whether it is viewed by the reader as an act of freedom or an act of power. This in turn has everything to do with the authority of the speaker. Paradoxically that authority grows the more the speaker is weakened and made vulnerable by the tensions he or she creates. By the same logic, it is diminished if the speaker protects himself or herself by the powers of language he or she can generate.

The political poem, in other words, proves in a single genre what is true of all poetry. The mover of the poem's action—the voice, the speaker—must be at the same risk from that action as every other component in the poem. If that voice is exempt, then the reader will hear it as omniscient; if it is omnisicient, it can still commend the ratio of power to powerlessness—but with the reduced authority of an observer.

It is impossible to be abstract about these things. You cannot prove a change in poetry by diagrams and numbers.

You cannot swear to it or set your clock by it. It is something which has to be deduced by instinct and practice, by reading and writing, often against the grain, often without certainty.

v.

I was certain of one thing: The confusion of the public and the political—although the cause of some real eloquence—could also make the genuinely radical poem less visible than it ought to be. And this frustrated me. I wanted to see the powerful public history of my own country joined by the private lives and solitary perspectives, including my own, which the Irish poetic tradition had not yet admitted to authorship. I wanted to see the effect of an unrecorded life—a woman in a suburban twilight under a hissing streetlight—on the prescribed themes of public importance.

Without this, I felt that the argument of the political poem might be limited to the public event and the communal interpretation of it. That was not the poem I wanted to write; it was not even the poem I wanted to read. Besides, I had a sense of an alternative. The eloquent and destabilizing effect of the private voice was already something I had observed in the best Irish poetry. And I was sure—if only the tradition would admit it as subject matter—that this could throw the conventional Irish political poem off-balance, offering it fresh perspectives and different alignments.

I already knew of a beautiful example. It came in a poem by Yeats called "Meditations in Time of Civil War." I had read it first as a teenager, just returned to boarding school after a visit to Galway. I could still see the stone walls and feel the roads rising and winding under the wheels of the car as I opened the book. Yeats had written his poem in Thoor Ballylee, his stone tower near the village of Gort, with the Slieve Aughty Mountains rising to the east and the stopped-up green water of a stream in front of it. The poem describes desolation, both within and without. It sets an ominous breakdown of public order—"that young soldier in his blood"—against the poet's own darkening perceptions. Throughout the first four sections of the poem these different realities seek each other out. Then in the fifth section they come together wonderfully:

> *An affable Irregular,*
> *A heavily-built Falstaffian man,*
> *Comes cracking jokes of civil war*
> *As though to die by gunshot were*
> *The finest play under the sun.*
>
> *A brown Lieutenant and his men,*
> *Half dressed in national uniform,*
> *Stand at my door, and I complain*
> *Of the foul weather, hail and rain,*
> *A pear tree broken by the storm.*
>
> *I count those feathered balls of soot*
> *The moor-hen guides upon the stream,*
> *To silence the envy in my thought;*
> *And turn towards my chamber, caught*
> *In the cold snows of a dream.*

The effect of this poem is wonderful and surprising. It takes a public reality of fixed meaning—a civil war fought in a rural setting—and destabilizes it through the intensity of a private world. Yeats meets the irregular at his front door and hears him cracking jokes about violence and death. Then he meets his opposite number, a lieutenant in the newly constituted national army, and complains to him, but this time about the natural violence of the weather.

At the end of the poem he is a pastoral poet, counting the moorhen's ducklings to suppress his own ambiguous feelings about the world of action, to silence "the envy in my thought." At the end of the poem also there is no doubt which is the paramount adventure: It is not the uniformed man or his opponent. Nor is it the natural world with its renewals and catastrophes. It is the vivid and divided world of the subject. Yeats had done what I had not even realized needed to be done that winter evening in the suburb. He had proposed a private world in a political poem—a world so volatile that it had collapsed and refreshed all the other apparently stable meanings in the poem.

To me this was the Irish political poem as it should be: fresh and startling, a lyric that could not be predicted or arranged. It made an encouraging sign about the real ability of an inner world to suffer the outer world so powerfully that history itself faltered before that gaze.

VI.

I have never felt I owned Irish history; I have never felt
entitled to the Irish experience. There have been Irish poets
who have written the political poem with exactly this sense of
ownership and entitlement. I doubt those credentials. It is a
weakness and not a strength of the Irish poetic tradition that it
encourages its poets to act as envoys of dispossession. The
political poem is not the report of a privileged witness. It is a
continuing action which revises, in some decisive way, the
perceived relation of power between an inner and outer
world. In the great dramas of language and vision these worlds
are rebalanced so that one can comment on the other rather
than crush it, so that the fracture in one annotates the wound
in the other.

During my twenties and thirties my interest in the political poem increased as my apparent access to it declined. I
sensed resistances around me. I was married; I lived in a suburb; I had small children. Permissions are neither spoken nor
conceded in a poetic discourse. Yet I knew that the permission for a suburban woman to write the Irish political poem
was neither allowed nor foreseen.

Irish poetry was male and bardic in formation. Its secrets
and inheritances divided it, even from the historical radical-
isms of the romantic movement. I had a deep suspicion of
those secrets. It was not just that by my having read American
poets like Elizabeth Bishop, my sense of the value and possi-

bility of being a guest editor at the historical process had been confirmed. It was something more.

I was skeptical of the very structure of the Irish poem. Its inherited voice, its authoritative stance, its automatic reflex of elegy—these given qualities, from a technical perspective, accrued too much power to the speaker to allow that speaker to be himself a plausible critic of power. And the power he had was a sweet and venerable one, with its roots deep in the flattery of princes and a bardic outrage at losing protected status for poets. It gave to Irish poets an authority long taken from or renounced by their British counterparts. The romantic poet was so suspicious of power that by 1820 he was safely on the road to a suspicion of poetry. The crisis of modernism was part of that outcome. The bardic poet, in his Irish manifestation, remained shuttered in an older faith: where poetry and privilege were inflexibly associated. Where, whatever the dispossession and humiliation of an outer world, maleness remained a caste system within the poem.

The shadow of bardic privilege still fell on the Irish poem when I was young. It was hard to question and harder to shift. Yet I knew I would have to do both if I wanted access to the political poem in Ireland. Nor did I simplify it into a question of gender and prejudice. It went far beyond that, to raise the whole issue of poetic authority: Women had for so long been a natural object relation for the Irish poem that women poets seemed less a new arrival in the literary tradition than a species of insubordination. It was as though a fixed part of the Irish poem had broken free and become volatile.

VII.

From the top windows at dusk I could see the steady lamps at the base of those hills and the flickering spiral of car headlights moving down it.

My children were born. I entered a world of routine out of which, slowly and mysteriously, a world of vision manifested itself. For all that, it was a commonsense and familiar world, a stretch of road with whitebeam trees and driveways where cars—the same, for all I knew, which had just moved down the hillside—returned at dusk and left first thing in the morning.

It was not just that I lived there. I learned to do that, and with full attention. Nor that I wrote poems there. I learned to do that too. The challenge was in making the connection, was in the care with which I perceived that the same tree and the daylight frost were not just recurrences but had the power to alter my view of the elegy, the pastoral and the nature poem.

One of the problems in making that connection was that all this was at a contradictory angle from the Irish poem as I first encountered it and had learned to write it. The Dublin I entered and published in as an undergraduate poet honored—in a small circle—its own view of the life of the poet. It was still, although this was less visible, recovering from the claim which the Literary Revival—and through it the national tradition—had laid on poetry. This claim dictated a certain se-

quence of importances and permissions for the Irish poem: for
its themes, its language and purpose. The political poem in
Ireland, by this definition, proved its Irishness by a subtle series of referential gestures. It was still weighed, as many post-
colonial instruments are, by a burden of proof: So that the
oppression could be further disproved, the oppressed must be
proved worthy over and over again. A stultifying series of
themes and tones lay heavily on the poem. And it offered, and
considered, no name for a poet who was about to live a life it
did not recognize as suitable for the Irish poem.

"The poetic image," writes Muriel Rukeyser, "is not a
static thing. It lives in time as does the poem." I wanted the
Irish poem to live in my time. The dial of a washing machine,
the expression in a child's face—these things were at eye level
as I bent down to them during the day. I wanted them to
enter my poems. I wanted the poems they entered to be Irish
poems. I was about to find that the poem in its time is a
register of resistances and difficulties which go well beyond
the intention and determination of any one poet. I was about
to find also that the politic of the poem—and also the political
poem—is a subtle and risky negotiation not only between
perceptions of power but between what is included in the
poem and what remains outside it. That relation between the
excluded and the included is the dominant politic of the
poem.

In my mid-twenties I had left an established literary
world for a neighborhood—real and figurative—where such
arguments and evaluations had no reality. If I had stayed,

there is at least a chance I might have renamed my life to comply with a forceful absence of any other name for it. Instead, to use Adrienne Rich's words, "I did begin to resist the apparent splitting of poet from woman, thinker from woman and to write what I feared was political poetry."

VIII.

My sense of the private life as a politic of its own was not fanciful. It had its source in my own sense of certain actions, certain commentaries as radical in context. In my twenties I had failed to see the connection between a young woman under a streetlamp and a horse blundering away in the dusk. I was determined it would not happen again.

The Irish poem, as it came from the nineteenth century, was marked and shaped by public perceptions. Its substance was eloquent and poignant. It canvassed the death of heroes and triumph against the odds. It ranged all the way from the street ballad about an execution to Samuel Ferguson's lament for Thomas Davis. It was the poem I heard as a child, the poetic decorum I inherited.

The problem was that this substance predicted a speaker. And the speaker of the poem—of the political poem, that is—was too often in sympathy with the substance, almost to the point where his viewpoint seemed to be created by it. Therefore, the planes and angles of the poem became flattened out. Where they should have jutted against a horizon, defining it by a sharp and challenging shape, they made a continuum with it. Or in other words, they fitted smoothly into the context of public opinion and assumption.

Even as I was debating this with myself, Irishwomen were writing poems where the private world was indeed a radical commentary. In her beautiful first book, *The Flower Master,* Medbh McGuckian, a poet from Belfast, had included a poem called "The Flitting." Its astonishing swerves and recoveries, its kaleidoscopic imagery created a perception of the exterior world which once again, as in Yeats's poem, testified to the power of the inner one:

> *I postpone my immortality for my children,*
> *Little rock roses, cushioned*
> *In long-flowering sea-thrift and metrics,*
> *Lacking elemental memories:*
> *I am well-earthed here as the digital clock,*
> *Its numbers flicking into place like overgrown farthings*
> *On a bank where once a train*
> *Ploughed like an emperor living out a myth*
> *Through the cambered flesh of clover and wild carrot.*

In the same way Eilean ni Chuilleanain could write in her first book, *Site of Ambush,* about "Light, weathered filterings/That shift under her feet" in a poem called "Darkening All the Strand" which infers the complex layerings of Irish culture. And in an eloquent poem called "The Pattern" a younger Dublin poet, Paula Meehan, in a poem which summons the life of her mother, inflects a world well beyond it:

And as she buffed the wax to a high shine
did she catch her own face coming clear?
Did she net a glimmer of her true self?
Did her mirror tell what mine tells me?
I have her shrug and go on
knowing history has brought her to her knees.

Of course, women poets in Ireland also inherited a powerful history and a persuasive construct. It would be foolish to deny it. The Irish nineteenth century reached out to them also, with its cause and its cadences. But there was a difference. Within a poetry inflected by its national tradition, women had often been double-exposed, like a flawed photograph, over the image and identity of the nation. The nationalization of the feminine, the feminization of the national, had become a powerful and customary inscription in the poetry of that very nineteenth-century Ireland. "Kathleen ni Houlihan!" exclaimed MacNeice. "Why/must a country like a ship or a car, be always/female?" A poetic landscape which had once been politicized through women was now politicized by them. The obstinate and articulate privacy of their lives was now writing the poem, rather than simply being written by it. If this did not make a new political poem, it at least constituted a powerful revision of the old one. As more and more poems by Irishwomen were written, it was obvious that something was happening to the Irish poem. It was what happens to any tradition when previously mute images within it come to awkward and vivid life, when the icons return to haunt the icon makers. That these disruptions had been necessary at all, and that they were awkward and painful when they happened, had something to do with the force of the national tradition.

IX.

Nationalism has an ironic effect on literature. In Irish poetry, at the end of the colonial nineteenth century, the national tradition operated as a powerful colonizer. It marked out value systems; it politicized certain realities and devalued others. To those it recognized and approved, it offered major roles in the story. To others, bit parts only.

Patrick Kavanagh got a bit part. And he knew it. Born in 1904 into a hard-pressed rural family, he represented a class which was falsely depicted and inaccurately politicized, both in Yeats's poetry and in the Literary Revival as a whole. He was acerbic about that misrepresentation. "When I came to Dublin," he writes in his *Self-Portrait,* "the Irish Literary Affair was still booming. It was the notion that Dublin was a literary metropolis and Ireland as invented and patented by Yeats, Lady Gregory and Synge, a spiritual entity. It was full of writers and poets and I am afraid I thought their work had the Irish quality."

Kavanagh was an obstinate lyric poet. His interests were not in social history but in the effects of language on vision—a concern which was disallowed by the expectations of the Literary Revival. Poets like Kavanagh were intended to exemplify the oppressions of Irish history by being oppressed.

197

Kavanagh resisted. He rejected a public role in favor of a private vision. It was a costly and valuable resistance—exemplary to poets like myself who have come later, and with different purposes, into that tradition.

Kavanagh was especially sensitive to the politicization of his own experience in previous Irish poetry. The Literary Revival was invested in a false pastoral. Against a heroic background the rural experience was both glamorized and distorted. Therefore, a poet such as Kavanagh was screen-tested in much the same way that Padraic Colum had been. They were meant to exemplify the oppressions of Irish history by being oppressed. "In those days in Dublin," Kavanagh writes, "the big thing besides being Irish was peasant quality. They were all trying to be peasants. They had been at it for years but I hadn't heard."

To be politicized in a poetic tradition, without having powers of expression or intervention to change the interpretation, is an experience Irish woman poets share with Kavanagh. Like them, he was part of the iconic structure of the Irish poem long before he became its author. Like them, his authorship involved him in iconic reversals and important shifts of emphasis. Like them, his previous objectification in the poem made him an important witness not just to his own themes but to the structure of a poetic tradition which had, in effect, silenced him. His poem "The Great Hunger" is an antipastoral. It sets out to explore and comment on a relation between man and nature which is neither the soft elegy of the British pastoral nor the social protest of the Irish one but marks out a painful and achieved connection between private suffering and all the complex references of local faith and sexual anguish and undependable vision:

> *The pull is on the traces, it is March*
> *And a cold black wind is blowing from Dundalk.*
> *The twisting sod rolls over on her back—*
> *The virgin screams before the irresistible sock.*
> *No worry on Maguire's mind this day*
> *Except that he forgot to bring his matches.*
> *"Hop back there Polly, hoy back, woa, wae."*
> *From every second field a neighbour watches*
> *With all the sharpened interest of rivalry.*
> *Yet sometimes when the sun comes through a gap*
> *These men know God the Father in a tree:*
> *The Holy Spirit is the rising sap,*
> *And Christ will be the green leaves that will come*
> *At Easter from the sealed and guarded tomb.*

x.

I wrote the political poem in Ireland because I was once politicized within it. By the same token, my womanhood—once its object and icon—became part of its authorship. These are difficult and awkward transitions. They in no way guarantee good poetry, but they have allowed me to take a different perspective on an old and hallowed craft. I am slow, for instance, to believe that the political poem can be written by a self that is not politicized, even radicalized. Once again I find it hard to accept that a radical self can function authoritatively in the political poem if the sexual self, which is part of it, remains conservative, exclusive and unquestioning of inherited authority.

In Ireland a paradox exists. A country with a wealth of themes encourages its poets, through a bardic past and a national tradition, to diminish them from political complexity to public statement. The best Irish poets have resisted this, and it needs to be resisted. Political poetry operates in the corridor between rhetoric and reality. It is an ineffective presence there if the poet provides the rhetoric while the reality remains outside the poem. How to draw the reality into the poem, and therefore into a subversive relation with the rhetoric, is the crucial question. But there are political poems written in Ireland, even today, in which the question is not even asked, let alone answered. This in turn prompts an even more central question: How can you subvert that relation if you have failed to subvert the tradition of expression with which you approach it?

The emergence of women poets in Ireland guarantees nothing. I want to be clear about that. They also use language; their language is open to scrutiny. But I have argued here, and I truly believe, that where icons walk out of the poem to become authors of it, their speculative energy is directed not just to the iconography which held them hostage but to the poem itself. This gives the woman poet such as myself the unique chance to fold language and history in on itself, to write a political poem which canvasses Irish history by questioning the poetic structures it shadowed. To dismantle, in other words, the rhetorical relationship by dismantling the poetic persona which supported it. And to seek the authority to do this not from a privileged or historic stance within the Irish poem but from the silences it created and sustained.

There is nothing restrictive in this. Nothing in my argument dishonors, or intends to dishonor, the good work done by male poets in Ireland. But I do intend to challenge the assumption, which is without intellectual rigor, that public poetry—whether it is about a scandal or a death or the situation in Northern Ireland—is necessarily political poetry. The two may overlap, but they are not the same. I also intend to challenge the central tenet of their confusion: the voice at the center of too many Irish poems which assumes that an inherited stance can stand in for an achieved poetic authority.

The confusion of the two has been damaging. It has created false acceptance and exclusions. It has opened the way for poems which are glibly concerned with violence, while on the other hand proposing that the life of a woman, as a theme, was incompatible with the purpose and seriousness of the political poem. Both these views owe something—even obliquely—to the shadowing of a poetic tradition by a national program which has sought, since the nineteenth century, to generate and recruit the political poem in Ireland. At its best the political poem can be an illuminating form. But in Ireland, above all, there is a need to remember that it is not exempt, by any virtue of contemporary reference, from the rules of vigilance and necessity which govern all poetic expression.

9.

I t is an evening in summer. The suburb is almost quiet. The Dublin hills are the last color they will be in the succession of colors they have been all day: a sort of charcoal violet. The trellises and sidewalls are well hidden with clematis and sweet pea. A neighbor's rectangle of rose garden is full of pastels, with one or two scarlets. A bicycle lies sideways on the ground. A child's plastic mug, with an orange beak on the lid of it, is thrown at the bottom of a step.

Everywhere you look there is evidence that this is a landscape of rapid change and ordinary survivals.

I am talking to a woman in the last light. I have just finished cutting the grass at the front, and we are outside, between her house and mine. We make that temporary shape that conversing neighbors often assume: not exactly settled into a discussion yet not ready to leave it either. She lives across the road from me. Her children are teenagers. Mine are still infants, asleep behind the drawn curtains in the rooms upstairs.

As we talk, I feel the shadow of some other meaning across our conversation, which is otherwise entirely about surface things. That it is high summer in my life, not in hers. That hers is the life mine will become, while mine is the life she has lost. And then the conversation ends. I turn to go in. I lift the bicycle and the mug.

That night something strange happens. I begin to make notes for a poem. I try to write it. As I do, I am aware of that split screen, that half-in-half perspective which is so connected with the act of writing. I am at a table at an open window. Outside the poem I can smell the sweet cut grass of the evening's task. Through the open doors of two rooms I can hear my children breathing. I see the poplars with their shadow-colored leaves. The connection between this world outside the poem and something it might become inside it is at first exciting, then difficult, then impossible to make. At some point I do what I have rarely done—at least not at such a preliminary stage of writing. I put down the pen. I leave my notes. I set aside the poem in the complete certainty that it will never be written.

Now let me stand back, from this distance, as I never could in the act of composition. Let me return to that night, to the page on the table, so as to look more exactingly at what it is I am trying to write, that I have not written, this poem that has failed to run what Frost called "a lucky course of events." Let me say, for the sake of argument, that the notes for the poem—although in fact they were nothing as coherent as this—involved three different elements: a suburb; the Dublin hills behind it; two women talking under a window where the children of one of them are asleep. Again, let me ask a question which is more self-conscious than any which could have proposed itself at that point: Which of these elements has given me so much difficulty that not only do I not write the poem, but I know in a very short time that it will not be written?

It is not the suburb; that much is certain. By now I have come to terms with the fact that a suburb is an awkward and unlikely theater for a poem. It is certainly true that this ordinary street, of young trees and younger children, has provided me with one of the most challenging components in a poetic theme: a devalued subject matter. It has given me an insight into the flawed permissions which surround the inherited Irish poem, in which you could have a political murder, but not a baby, and a line of hills, but not the suburbs under them. Nevertheless, I think of these as problems rather than obstructions. They test me; they do not silence me. They make it clear that the tense relation between the suburb and a societal perception of it is only a restatement of the connection between the complexity of any theme and its caricature.

Then there are the Dublin hills. All through that conversation they have been collecting shadows. By now it must be obvious that I am making a deliberate artifice: arguing as though the elements of a poem were separable and clear units, some of which may be inspected for obstructive tendencies, others of which can be considered free of them. Of course they cannot. But allowing for the artifice, let me look more closely at these hills.

Outside the poem they make a half circle on the southwest of our horizon. Their low curve is marked by soft colors. Their contour hides the rising of the river Liffey—a trickle among ling and bracken and heather—which made the city. Inside the poem the two blunt syllables of the word *Dublin* and the poignant signaling which the local makes to the national are presences and inferences which must be reckoned with. But by now, as an Irish poet and a woman, I have come face-to-face with these things. The truths of womanhood and the defeats of a nation have drawn nearer to each other in my work; they make an improbable intersection. Nevertheless, I sense they may yet inform each other. I already know that for me anyway, the only possible dialogue with the idea of a nation will be a subversive one. And even this will not be easy.

The suburb. The Dublin hills. They are not the problem. They offer challenges, not silences. And the challenges simply serve to illustrate that a place should find its poem, a time its expression—things which most poets know anyway. For all the difficulties, they hold out the possibility of such discoveries—of that glamour of meaning which Pasternak describes happening in the Petersburg poems of Blok: "Adjectives without a noun, predicates without a subject, alarm, excitement, hide-and-seek, abruptness, whisking shadows—how well this style accorded with the spirit of a time, itself secretive, hermetic, underground, only just out of the cellars, and still using the language of conspiracy, the spirit of a time and of a tale in which the chief character was the town and the street was the chief event."

It is in the foreground of the poem that the difficulties exist. That the poem falters. Where the women stand and talk—deep within that image is, I know, another image. The deeper image is that shadow, the aging woman, the argument that the body of one woman is a prophecy of the body of the other. Here, at the very point where I am looking for what Calvino calls "that natural rhythm, as of the sea or the wind, that festive light impulse," the exact opposite happens. I cannot make her real; I cannot make myself real. I cannot make the time we are happening in real, so that the time I fear can also happen.

But why? The answer to that question, which was hardly formulated then, is part of the reason for my argument. Then I was merely confused; even now I may not be clear. And yet I sensed, hidden in the narrative distance between myself and this theme of aging women, some restriction, some thickening and stumbling. Writing a poem is so instinctive that it can be almost impossible, in the actual moment, to separate an aesthetic difficulty from a personal limitation. But this was different. I could not write these women. I could not write the misadventure of time which was happening to them in an ordinary Dublin twilight. That I could not write it was nothing new. What unsettled me was that—at some level I barely understood—neither did I feel free to imagine it.

Why does the page lie on the table by the window? Why are the table deserted and the pen to one side of it? Why am I about to make an unwritten poem into this small biography of the silences it retreated into? The answer is as complicated and elusive as anything I know and understand about poetry. I could say that through a failed poem, I stumbled on a field of force. Even then I will have given only part of the answer. As the poem hesitated, as I failed to make those women real, two things happened: I lost the poem I might have written, and I found—although this was not clear until later—a place of fixities and resistances where the lineaments of a tradition meet the intention of an individual poet. Something had shifted. Something had brought me to a place of change. I thought of Adrienne Rich's words about her own revision of her working methods: "Like the novelist who finds that his characters begin to have a life of their own and to demand certain experiences, I find that I can no longer go to write a poem with a neat handful of materials and express those materials according to a prior plan."

Plans. Materials. These are not words readily associated

with poetry. Then again, what I felt that summer night was outside my experience as a poet. I needed to analyze my failure. Was it technical? Or imaginative? Related to the tradition? Or merely part of my circumstance? The more I thought about it, the more drawn I was towards the interior of the poem—that structure which, for every generation of poets, is a new mystery. Changes to it are rarely visible; fixities within it are hard to describe. Enormous questions loomed up. Was it possible that the precedents and customs of the poetic tradition were fixed in such a way—like signs facing south on a road due west—that they could mark the interior of the poem with some inbuilt resistance to a woman aging in it? No sooner did I ask the question than I had a sense of its vastness. No sooner did I try to answer it than I had an equivalent sense of how frail and makeshift the language of poetic practice has become in our generation, in contrast with the formidable extrapoetic definitions of it that exist beyond the poem. Then again, a working poet, struggling to make sense of a complex tradition in a time of change, cannot be a theorist or an ideologue. The questions I asked and the answers I attempted, and everything that follows from them in this account, did not come from any such source. They came simply and inevitably—to use Stevens's words—from "my desire to add my own definitions to poetry's many existing definitions."

II.

I want a poem I can grow old in. I want a poem I can die in. It is a human wish, meeting language and precedent at the point of crisis. What is there to stop me? What prevents me taking up a pen and recording in a poem the accurate detail of time passing, which might then become a wider exploration of its meaning? My daughters' shadows in the garden, for instance, now grown longer than my own.

It is not so simple. The assumption is still made, is a sort of leftover from romanticism, that a poem is a free space within which the poet exercises options comparable to those outside. The reality is different. Outside the poem the poet is indeed free, does indeed have choices. Once he or she is inside it, these choices are altered and limited in several specific ways. Let me say, for the sake of argument, that a woman poet is writing at a window, that she is trying to formalize something that has happened to her, that she writes words on the page, crosses them out and begins again. She has now entered the poem and is absorbed by the difficulties and possibilities within it. By these various actions she has made an important alteration in the fixity or freedom of her position: She is now not only the author of the action but an image within it. This changes things. Image systems within poetry—of which she is now a part—are complex, referential and historic. Within them are stored not simply the practices of a tradition but the precedent which years of acquaintance with, and illumination by, that tradition offers to the poet at that moment of absorption in the poem.

Let me now put this abstraction back into the narrative I began with. I believe the unwritten poem of that summer night prompted me to continue—I had already begun to move in that direction—a journey of doubt and discovery which would bring me to the heart of poetry, as I understood it. There I found, as all poets do, the treasurable inscriptions and fixities which are the powerful outcome of tradition and precedent. There again, as all poets do, I struggled to make sense of them, and as all poets must, I determined to make some transaction with them which would recognize their wisdom, while still allowing me to experiment in my work. Increasingly—I am now greatly simplifying these processes of doubt and discovery—I came to understand that one of these signs would not yield to such a transaction, could not easily be made an informative part of my work and might even be part of the reason I had felt such a resistance within theme and language that summer evening.

If I had to name this inscription, I would say that the sexual and erotic were joined in a powerful sign which marked the very center of poetry. I knew without yet being able to reason it out that this was one of the oldest, most commanding fixities in poetry, responsible for the beauty of the erotic object in the poem. But also for its silence and agelessness. And I sensed—but this is getting well ahead of the argument—that this sign might be the very one which was responsible for those resistances deep within the tradition which I was certain I had encountered that summer night. In its mixture of image and emblem, of desire and expression, it took a mortal woman and fixed her in a certain relation within the poem. By so doing, it emphasized her ornamental qualities and disallowed her mortality. And I knew two other things as well—instinctively, and without hesitation: that I could not make this sign and that I would have to define it. And it is this last which I will make some attempt at now.

I am well aware that words such as *sexual* and *erotic* have—in the world outside the poem—daunting engagements with the social, the psychological, the sociological. These are not my concern and are, in any case, well outside my competence. Nevertheless, in order to get to their meaning in the poem, I will attempt some makeshift definition of their meaning outside it. For most people, if the sexual act is the unambiguous physical union, the erotic is something different. While the *Oxford English Dictionary* describes it merely as something "tending to arouse sexual love or desire," its existence in culture and reference is both more oblique and more mysterious. Even its common caricature as a shoe or a silk garment or a piece of leather cannot hide its poignant complexity: that it is the outcome of an imaginative sexual world—in which fear and awe are powerful presences—which may remain unexpressed, or even rebuffed, by the act itself. That it comes into focus in that hinterland of perception where sense and spirit are wounded and fractured. That it is at once the object of desire and the reminder of such a fracture.

These definitions are replaceable with a hundred more, and even then they will be contentious. But in the day-to-day world of poetic practice I believe these broad terms sharpen and narrow and gather a more precise meaning. They cease to be merely a dialect of our malaise. They acquire references to, and engagements with, forceful and customary parts of poetic expression. For all that, an exact definition remains thoroughly elusive. I could start by proposing the functions of these words, rather than their meaning. The erotic object, for instance, is most often part of the image system of the poem, while the sexualization of it is integral to the poet's perspective and stance; it therefore becomes part of voice and argument. In a poem about the silks a woman is wearing, written by her lover, the silks become the mute erotic object, while the perception of them as beautiful and exciting becomes part of the poet's perspective in the poem.

The problem with this neat and blunt way of looking at things is that it sweeps away, in a few words, the crucial fact about the sexual and the erotic in poetry: that their fusion is so powerful not simply because the erotic object, as an image, is distanced and controlled by the sexual perspective of the poet, although it is. Nor that we see in this fusion the appropriation of the powerless by the powerful, although we do. The crucial aspect of the relation between the sexual and the erotic in this context is that the erotic object is possessed not by the power of sexuality but by the power of expression. The erotic object therefore becomes a beautiful mime of those forces of expression which have silenced it. Its reason for being there may seem to be that it is both beautiful and yearned for, but at a deeper level it becomes a trophy of the forces which created it, not simply because it is sexualized but because it is sexualized within a triumphant and complex act of poetry.

III.

Where did I find this fusion of the sexual and the erotic proposed, and how did I decipher it? The answer is clear enough. I read poems. I thought about them. I tried to define their meaning as I came to write my own. The light on the page and the poem was a variable: It could be my interest in a particular form, or a sense of time passing, or pleasure in another poet's use of language. The landscape around me as I read was a summer darkness or a hill frost or a child crying my name or a telephone ringing.

The things I found as I read and wrote intrigued and excited me. But when I came to describe them—then as now—my definitions were halting and unscientific and incomplete. And not only halting but fallible and idiosyncratic as well. I read poems other people might not have read. I read them in contexts which were private rather than communal. And so I have no exact words of explanation for how charmed and troubled I was by a poem like "Upon Julia's Clothes" by Robert Herrick:

Whenas in silks my Julia goes.
Then, then (methinks) how sweetly flows
That liquefaction of her clothes.
Next, when I cast mine eyes and see
That brave vibration each way free;
Oh how that glittering taketh me!

Who could deny it? Robert Herrick, the goldsmith's apprentice and vicar, whose life-span reached from the Armada
to the Restoration, could put together a seamless music. His
six-liner is eloquent and forceful. It is also a diagram of the
appropriation of the erotic by the sexual and of both by a
power of expression which is self-aware and triumphant and
whose assertion is a prime mover in the poem, a shape
changer shifting pronouns and disassembling metaphor before
our eyes. The erotic object—those silks turning to water and
light—is fixed in a relation to the more volatile parts of the
poem. The outcry of the final line, where the possessor is
possessed, is at once a bright irony and a coded pastoral. The
impression the poem leaves is of power and possession, ren-
dered as delight by the decorum of language. It is an impression made more vivid by the use—in a tiny work space—of
me and *my;* the ascribing of vision and perception to the
speaker and only movement to the spoken-of; the perfect,
rapid cadence and the final solipsistic cry. And all the while
Julia and the silks are silent and still.

There are problems with all this. To start with, I am
using a language which is itself a construct of hindsight. It may

214

serve to highlight the text, but it does no justice to the way I
first read a poem such as this. It implies sharp practice, a sort of
loitering with intent in books and anthologies, keeping a
sharp eye out for unwary images and references. Almost the
opposite is true. I came on these poems with delight. I read
them. I remembered them. Only later did I reconsider them
in the light of my own work and my own hesitant progress
towards a voice that was mine. And once I began to reconsider, I could see these tropes and figures as both persuasive
and unsettling. And then I read more and with a growing
sense of their recurrence in the traditional poem. And once
again this was the tradition as I had known it, as both a young
woman and a scholar. The works of the British canon. The
poems read by the poets who wrote poems which were read
by other poets. In such downright ways traditions are made.
In such clear and yet complex ways their legislation is
enacted:

> *Fair youth, beneath the trees, thou canst not leave*
> *Thy song, nor ever can those trees be bare;*
> *Bold Lover, never, never canst thou kiss*
> *Though winning near the goal—yet do not grieve;*
> *She cannot fade though thou hast not thy bliss,*
> *For ever wilt thou love, and she be fair!*

At first sight Keats's lines from "Ode on a Grecian Urn"
seem to contradict the fusion of the erotic and the sexual. A
closer look reveals an astonishing and intense poise of these
elements and a candid appraisal of both as creatures of the

expressive. It is simply that the parts are dismantled and put together in a fresh and strange way. The young man in decorative chase on the side of the urn has the sexual perspective which seeks to possess; the maiden has the erotic task of being simply mute and beautiful. The poet has assumed the expressive power which controls the act of desire, the intent to possess, which can leave both in that timeless posture of seeking and restraining, while the true possession of either is assumed by art rather than sexuality. And thus—through a wonderful elliptical syntax and the musical vocative of the last line—the elements of the sexualized erotic are revealed to be what they truly are in the poem of the tradition: not a drama of desire but a drama of expression.

IV.

What if those components were taken apart and reworked? What if the elements which made up a narrow and intense convention were disassembled and changed and put back into the poem? The very reason I wrote this is to give an account of how I came on those questions. Of how I tried to answer them. And yet the arguments involved are so difficult that to put them forward at all is to feel at times like a physicist searching for black vacuums in outer space which can be deduced only by equations which rule out other possibilities. And so to turn the difficulties into some kind of accessible drama, I intend to propose them for a moment as surrealisms, as a series of what-ifs and whether-nots.

Suppose it were possible to encounter the poems of the

past not as finished forms but as actions we could reverse. Suppose I could gather these objects from those poems: the light in the jewel, the silk of the skirt, the skin of the shepherdess and the hair of the nymph. What would I have collected? I would have—I have entered the surreal now—a series of fixed and glittering objects. Which could not age. Which could not suffer.

Now let me extend the fabulous element of this argument. What if their age-old poetic connection with the sexualized were broken? What if the silk reverted to honest cloth rather than his mistress's skirt? What if I took them up and set them down in poems I wrote—in a landscape which was sensory and not erotic. The answer must be that they would no longer be erotic objects. And I would be a woman poet in a poignant place: a magnetic field where the created returns as creator. A place I already knew.

v.

My mid-thirties were a time of delay and puzzlement and reflection. A time when I stood talking to a neighbor on a summer evening and went upstairs to write a poem that was never written. Unspoken subjects deep within ordinary conversation. Unwritten poems on a table by the window. All poets have testing times. This was mine.

The apprenticeship of any poet—the years of learning and discouragement and skill—is a mystery. Not because of its importance but because so much gets lost. What remains the same is the struggle with language and the encounter with precedent. What changes is the detail of the encounter: Keats putting on a white shirt to write. Akhmatova's friend memorizing her work in a back garden in Leningrad. Plath turning on the Pifco coffeepot at 4:00 A.M. in the last month of her life.

I began to write poetry, in a serious way, in my late teens. I knew I was Irish. I knew I was a woman. But at the oilskin tablecloth where I laid out my books to work in the evening it sometimes seems to me, looking back, that I was sexless, Victorian, a product of nineteenth-century ideas. I worked for the clear line, the pure stanza. Certainly at first I had no idea how to include the awkward, jagged reality in the decorums I admired.

As I wrote more, as I discovered the sensory world, as I saw the power of language to edit it, I changed. It was not so much, at first, that I wrote differently. But when I read, it was as if I saw something out of the corner of my eye, which disappeared, which I caught sight of again. A shepherdess in Spenser. The rustling silks in "The Eve of St. Agnes." A nymph. These mute objects stayed at the edges of my vision. As my life did.

And in the poems of my youth—this must be true of the majority of young poets—my sexual sense was conventional. My erotic sense lay beneath it like a reef beneath water. And however radical my hopes as a poet, they could have remained trapped in that conventional sexuality had it not been for one thing: I married. I moved to the suburbs. I made a home in a place where the writ of poetry did not run. I was now a suburban woman, and although I might find myself as a minor character in a novel, I would not find myself in a poem unless I wrote it. And then my children were born, and suddenly those objects which had caught my eyes and disappeared, and yet remained on the edges of my vision when I was a young poet, came to the center of my world.

As my children woke, as they slept, a visionary landscape scrolled around me. It was not made by my children, although the bright digits of their gloves and their plastic mugs littered it. It was made by my body. As I moved through a world of small tasks and almost endless routines, the red mug and the blue glove crept out of their skins. They were not erotic objects; almost the reverse. They were not emblems of the power of the body or the triumph of expression. They were annunciations of what my body had created and what, with every hour, and every day, it was losing. When I stood on my front doorstep on a summer night, the buddleia and the lamplight glossing the hedge were not just visible to me. I saw them with my body. And the sight of my body was clear and different and intense. What was seen by it was made both more clear and more ominous because I could not see it that way forever. And for some reason, although it was a radical difference in my life, I trusted this way of seeing. I believed what was seen. It was—at certain definable moments in that ordinary world—that I felt I stood in the place of myth and lyric and vision. "It is," says Eliade, "the irruption of the sacred into the world, an irruption narrated in the myths, that establishes the world as a reality."

I have tried to create here a diagram of one adventure in

perception. In doing so, I am making conscious and sche-
matic what lay under the surface of that perception. I am putting a chronology, a shape, a dialectic on what was never so
exact. And yet there is accuracy in it. My children grew. Tennis rackets replaced mugs and toys. Gradually the visionary
world hid itself in the world of detail which only occasionally
gives way to it. But I had learned something. I knew—like a
traveler who returns from a land that is not yet on the map—
that I had lived in a sensory world so intense that it had
marked me. From then on I was conscious of an ill-defined
but important relation between the erotic object of the male
poem and the sensory world I had lived in, with its colors and
edges and enticements. And it seemed to me, in terms of my
own poetry, that whereas the erotic object inflected the
power of expression and was fixed by the senses, these sensory
objects revealed a world suffered by the senses but not owned
by them. And yet my line of reasoning at this stage was so
halting and uncertain that to follow it further would be to see
it disappear. I was faltering between perceptions. Building an
argument, then losing the line of it. Coming to conclusions,
then backing away. Only slowly did a story begin to emerge.
Only gradually did I come to believe I could tell it.

VI.

I want to look briefly at four poems by women—one of
them my own—so as to illustrate and press these points. I intend them as quickly taken snapshots of the ways women poets
are rewriting the old fixities of the sexual and erotic, are reas-

sembling a landscape where subject and object are differently politicized, where expression, far from being an agent of power, may be an index of powerlessness. I intend them to suggest, however sketchily, the distances and differences which open up when these traditional elements are disassembled.

In the last month of her life Sylvia Plath was living in a flat in Fitzroy Road in London. I remember that winter. I shared a garden flat in South Dublin with my sister. It was my first winter out of school, and I was eighteen years of age, a student at Trinity College. The house in which we had the flat was on a leafy road, hardly five minutes by bus from the center of town. It backed onto a narrow garden which led, by a makeshift path, to the Dodder River, a tributary of the Liffey. Dublin was still a town. There was something uncityish still about these outlying roads, which were only slowly turning into suburbs. That January I studied Keats and Byron. I wrote poems, but in a faltering way. What I remember most clearly is the stone windowsill at garden level, smoking with frost in an early dark. It was cold in a way I had never known before in Ireland, a relentless, killing cold.

Sylvia Plath's flat was minimalist, put together in the pre-Christmas haste and fragmentation of that time. The young woman who had once written about wanting a house with "spreading apple trees, fields, a cow and a vegetable garden" was now older and lived in the heart of a city. Al Alvarez described her in that setting: "She had deliberately kept the place bare: rush matting on the floor, a few books, bits of Victoriana and cloudy blue glass on the shelves."

Against that background she set a poem called "Balloons." It is dated February 6, the same day on which she wrote "Edge," her lovely, scalding farewell to life, with its funerary images and odd lilt of peace. Five days later she was dead.

BALLOONS

Since Christmas they have lived with us
Guileless and clear
Oval soul-animals
Taking up half the space
Moving and rubbing on the silk

Invisible air drifts
Giving a shriek and a pop
When attacked, then scooting to rest, barely trembling.
Yellow cathead, blue fish—
Such queer moons we live with

Instead of dead furniture!
Straw mats, white walls
And those travelling
Globes of thin air, red, green
Delighting

The heart like wishes or free
Peacocks blessing
Old ground with a feather
Beaten in starry metals.
Your small

Brother is making
His balloon squeak like a cat.
Seeming to see
A funny pink world he might eat on the other side of it,
He bites

Then sits
Back, fat jug
Contemplating a world clear as water,
A red
Shred in his little fist

This poem occurs in an original and powerful sensory world, poised somewhere between treasure and danger. Obviously—since they are unconnected to a sexual perspective—the balloons are not erotic. Yet as images they operate in that territory where the strongest love poems also take hold: in a place where spirit and sense are seeking each other out. And in some ways, by being intensely sensory—highly colored, richly perceived and presences in the world of the body which children evoke—the balloons are preerotic. What distinguishes them so powerfully from the erotic object of the traditional poem is that they signify not the desire of the body or the triumph of expression but the fragility of the one and the intense vulnerability of the other. And far from being possessed by the perspective which creates them, the balloons are set free within the poem as they might be outside it: to ride out a current of association and surrealism which ends in their destruction and the end of the poem. And the balloon which ends up as "A red Shred" has had, by the end, a joyous, rapid mutation: has been a cat head and a globe, has been held by a child and has squeaked like a cat. Above all, it has not been fixed. The dominant impression left by the poem is of an imagination which has surrendered generously to the peril and adventure of the sensory moment, whose powers of expression have not been confirmed by it and whose bodily vulnerability has been increased by it. Most intriguingly of all, the poem glances over a reference which—with its resonance of ornament and myth—could easily be part of the erotic signposting of the traditional poem. But instead of that, the poem inflects the peacock differently. It becomes the beautiful, lucky emblem of a free heart and a blessed place. "[W]ith a feather/Beaten in starry metals." As we drown in the image, a pastoral convention flashes before our eyes, but in reverse: Instead of a natural world artificialized and regretted from the vantage point of the court, the artifice of the peacock is glimpsed through the beautiful lens of a natural and sensory world.

When Keats wrote "The Eve of St. Agnes," he assembled an elaborate series of word pictures, against which a cardboard-thin dramatic action unfolds. The characters are stock characters; the fable is a predictable mix of medieval nostalgia and Regency romance. The great beauty and force of the piece lie in the skilled distances and vowel melodies, the true stanzaic dramas and the clairvoyant sense of the erotic moment as a still life:

> *. . . her vespers done,*
> *Of all its wreathèd pearls her hair she frees;*
> *Unclasps her warmèd jewels one by one;*
> *Loosens her fragrant bodice; by degrees*
> *Her rich attire creeps rustling to her knees.*

The wonderful, drawn-out vowels—wreathèd/frees/ degrees/creeps/knees—create a static and delayed mood. They make a pageant of the stanza. Against that background the pearls are erotic objects, an integral part of the drama which unfolds.

How different are the pearls of another poem by the marvelous British poet Carol Ann Duffy. The poem is called "Warming Her Pearls" and is an unsparing evocation of power and desire between women. I quote it here in its entirety:

WARMING HER PEARLS

> *Next to my own skin, her pearls. My mistress*
> *bids me wear them, warm them, until evening*
> *when I'll brush her hair. At six I place them*
> *round her cool, white throat. All day I think of her*
>
> *resting in the Yellow Room, contemplating silk*
> *or taffeta, which gown tonight? She fans herself*
> *whilst I work willingly, my slow heat entering*
> *each pearl. Slack on my neck, her rope.*

She's beautiful. I dream about her
in my attic bed; picture her dancing
with tall men, puzzled by my faint, pervasive scent
beneath her French perfume, her milky stones.

I dust her shoulders with a rabbit's foot,
watch the soft blush seep through her skin
like an indolent sigh. In her looking-glass
my red lips part as though I want to speak.

Full moon. Her carriage brings her home. I see
her every movement in my head. . . . Undressing,
taking off her jewels, her slim hand reaching
for the case, slipping naked into bed, the way

she always does. . . . And I lie here awake,
knowing her pearls are cooling even now
in the room where my mistress sleeps. All night
I feel their absence and I burn.

"Warming Her Pearls" is a bold subversion of the sexualized erotic, a lyric which reassembles the love poem so that it becomes, like handwriting in a mirror, a menacing reversed message: The speaker is powerless, while the object of her affections has a power which puts her well beyond possession by either desire or expression. The pearls are not the fixed object of Keats's poem. They are the flawed, wounded and ironized erotic object of the traditional poem, but this time held in common between the women, rather than perceived as a fixed object, distanced from the speaker. In addition, they have a human warmth—they are milky, heated—which removes them once again from the glittering and unmortal objects of the traditional love poem. Just as this poem disassembles elements of the traditional love poem, so the subject-object relations come apart as well. The pearls are part of the disassembling. Where Keats's pearls happen at a great distance, these are heated, dangerous, ambiguous. Where the erotic object of the traditional love poem—such as Julia's silks—witnesses the orderly progression of power between poet and perception, the pearls restate the fixed decorum of that relation by deliberately suggesting a breakdown of power within the poem. Far from signaling controlled distance, they inflect the anguish and ugliness of control itself.

The erotic object defied nature. Timeless and ageless, it lay in the amber of the poem. If it were disassembled, a question might arise which said: What exactly is the nature poem? Certainly it has progressed and changed, evolved and revolved around the powerful disruptions which define poetry in its time. The romantic movement, being one of these, reworked the idea that the nature poem stated a series of moral recognitions between the inner and outer world. Wordsworth's midnight cliff. Shelley's west wind.

One of the exciting outcomes of women disassembling the sexual and erotic in poetry is a different nature poem. Different, above all, in its interpretation of what nature is. "Mock Orange" by Louise Gluck is a new kind of nature poem. Once again its starting point is a disassembly of familiar elements of the sexualized erotic. A woman speaks in the poem. A woman who might once—like the pearls—have been spoken of. She does not consider nature an outward sign of an inward grace. Quite the opposite. She considers the wound between spirit and sense almost intolerable, and that nature, far from healing it, has actually authorized it. She speaks bitterly of the betrayals of the sexual act, of the deceptions of nature in the scent and grace of the mock orange. As she deploys deceptive ecstasy as a metaphor for deceiving nature, age-old stabilities of poetic convention—nymphs, dryads, obedient Muses—seem to take flight, like wood spirits evicted from a forest. As the action develops, a superb and radical restatement of the nature poem forms before our eyes:

MOCK ORANGE

It is not the moon, I tell you.
It is these flowers
lighting the yard.

I hate them.
I hate them as I hate sex,
the man's mouth
sealing my mouth, the man's
paralyzing body—

And the cry that always escapes,
the low, humiliating
premise of union—

In my mind tonight
I hear the question and pursuing answer
fused in one sound
that mounts and mounts and then
is split into the old selves,
the tired antagonisms. Do you see?
We were made fools of.
And the scent of mock orange
drifts through the window.

How can I rest?
How can I be content
when there is still
that odor in the world?

One of the fascinations of this poem is that its voice is not simply the achieved voice of the narrator; it can also be heard as the cry of the erotic object—that silenced, paralyzed, gagged object—finding air and expression and dissent from its age-long role as servant of desire and trophy of the power of poetry. The narrator of this poem does not flinch from the volatile mix of the sexual and erotic, but once again they are radically disassembled. The erotic object is now the speaker. The sexualizing perspective is now the substance of the rebuke. The powers of nature so often celebrated and invoked in the traditional love poem are accused and reproached.

By the end of my thirties I had reached some peace with my work. The fragments and contradictions which had tormented my youth as a poet—issues of Irishness and of wom-

anhood and the more subtle issues of an ethical identity—
were beginning to find some repose. Yet in some area of my
mind that failure remained: that inability to write the aging
body. And in some part of my memory remained also those
glowing, broken images of the first years of the children's
lives: the luminous glove, the bright mug.

And yet stating it like this gives an ingenuity and symmetry to what was barely recognized. There were yearnings
and false starts. Starings out of the window. A sense of a theme
just out of sight. Barely more than that. To bring all this to the
light of day now and present it as argument and answer runs
the risk of falsifying it. And yet I need some construct to explain how—slowly and unsurely—I began to move towards
that theme.

I make these remarks as a preliminary to a poem I wrote
about a black lace fan my mother had given me, which my
father had given her in a heat wave in Paris in the thirties. It
would be wrong to say I was clear, when I wrote this poem,
about disassembling an erotic politic. I was not. But I was
aware of my own sense of the traditional erotic object—in
this case the black fan—as a sign not for triumph and acquisi-
tion but for suffering itself. And without having words for it,
I was conscious of trying to divide it from its usual source of
generation: the sexualized perspective of the poet. To that
extent I was writing a sign which might bring me closer to
those emblems of the body I had seen in those visionary years,
when ordinary objects seemed to warn me that the body

might share the world but could not own it. And if I was not conscious of taking apart something I had been taught to leave well alone, nevertheless, I had a clear sense of—at last—writing the poem away from the traditional erotic object towards something which spoke of the violations of love, while still shadowing the old context of its power. In other words, a back-to-front love poem.

THE BLACK LACE FAN
MY MOTHER GAVE ME

It was the first gift he ever gave her
buying it for five francs in the Galeries
in pre-war Paris. It was stifling.
A starless drought made the nights stormy.

They stayed in the city for the summer.
They met in cafés. She was always early.
He was late. That evening he was later.
They wrapped the fan. He looked at his watch.

She looked down the Boulevard des Capucines.
She ordered more coffee. She stood up.
The streets were emptying. The heat was killing.
She thought the distance smelled of rain and lightning.

These are wild roses appliquéd on silk by hand,
darkly picked, stitched boldly, quickly.
The rest is tortoiseshell and has the reticent
clear patience of its element. It is

a worn-out underwater bullion and it keeps,
even now, an inference of its violation.
The lace is overcast as if the weather
it opened for and offset had entered it.

The past is an empty café terrace.
An airless dusk before thunder. A man running.
And no way now to know what happened then—
none at all—unless of course you improvise:

The blackbird on this first sultry morning
in summer, finding buds, worms, fruit
feels the heat. Suddenly she puts out her wing.
The whole, full, flirtatious span of it.

VII.

It stands to reason that the project of the woman poet—
connected as it is by dark bonds to the object she once was—
cannot make a continuum with the sexualized erotic of the
male poem. The true difference women poets make as authors of the poem is in sharp contrast with the part they were
assigned as objects in it. As objects they were once images. As
images they were eroticized and distanced. A beautiful and
compelling language arose around them. In pastorals, lyrics,
elegies, odes they were shepherdesses, mermaids, nymphs.
The accoutrements of their persons became images within
images; their jewels, silks, skin, eyes became tropes and figures, at once celebrated and silenced.

It has been my argument that in a real and immediate

sense, when she does enter upon this old territory where the erotic and sexual came together to inflect the tradition, the woman poet is in that poignant place I spoke of, where the subject cannot forget her previous existence as object. There are aesthetic implications to this, but they are not separable from the ethical ones. And the chief ethical implication it seems to me is that when a woman poet deals with these issues of the sexual and the erotic, the poem she writes is likely to have a new dimension. It can be an act of rescue rather than a strategy of possession. And the object she returns to rescue, with her newly made Orphic power and intelligence, would be herself: a fixed presence in the underworld of the traditional poem. It is easy enough to see that her dual relation to the object she makes—as both creator and rescuer—shifts the balance of subject and object, lessens the control and alters perspectives within the poem.

I have also argued that far from making a continuum, the contemporary poem as written by women can actually separate the sexual and erotic, and separate, also, the sexual motif from that of poetic expression. And that when a woman poet does this, a circuit of power represented by their fusion is disrupted. The erotic object can be rescued and restored: from silence to expression, from the erotic to the sensory. When this happens, beautiful, disturbing tones are free to enter the poem. Poetry itself comes to the threshold of changes which need not exclude or diminish the past but are bound to reinterpret it.

Above all—and this was what chiefly drew me towards

the whole complex process of argument and exploration—
this disassembling of a traditional fusion offered a radical and
exciting chance to restate time in the poem. If the erotic object was indeed part of a drama of expression rather than a
drama of desire, then it was also a signal of powers which
were expressive and poetic more than they were sexual. As
such the erotic object had to do justice to the powers it re-
flected. It had to be a perfect moon to that sun. It could not be
afflicted by time or made vulnerable by decay. It could not
age. If this object—whether it was silk or pearls or a tree or a
fan—were reclaimed by the woman poet and set down in a
sensory world which inflected the mortality of the body,
rather than the strength of the expressive mind, then, by just
such an inflection, it would be restored to the flaws of time.

And here at last, it seemed to me, right across my path
lay the shadow that had fallen across my poem that summer
night. In the poem of the tradition the erotic object was a
concealed boast, a hidden brag about the powers of poetry
itself: that it could stop time. That it could fend off decay.
Therefore, I—and other women poets—as we entered our
own poems found an injunction already posted there. Inasmuch as we had once been objects—or objectified—in those
poems, we had been perfect and timeless. Now, as authors of
poems ourselves, if we were to age or fail or be simply mortal,
we would have to do more than simply write down those
things as themes or images. We would have to enter the interior of the poem and reinscribe certain powerful and custom-

ary relations between object and subject. And be responsible for what we did.

VIII.

I have come to believe that the woman poet is an emblematic figure in poetry now in the same way the modernist and romantic poets once were. And for the same reasons. Not because she is awkward and daring and disruptive but because—like the modernist and romantic poets in their time—she internalizes the stresses and truths of poetry at a particular moment. Her project therefore is neither marginal nor specialist. It is a project which concerns all of poetry, all that leads into it in the past and everywhere it is going in the future.

But it cuts both ways. Unlike a poet such as Adrienne Rich, to whom I feel so much indebtedness, I believe the past is the profound responsibility of the woman poet, as it was of the romantic and modernist poets in their time. She did not make it, and Adrienne Rich, more than any poet in my lifetime, has had the courage to address this. Nevertheless, if the woman poet makes a new custom and a different sign, she is not, by that process alone, free of her engagement with the old signs. She must renegotiate a position with the poetic past which is appropriate to her project and faithful to her imaginative freedoms. But which also is generous to that past and delicate in manner to the spirit of a tradition which sustained her.

This is intensely problematic. The sign I have written

about here, which concerns eroticism and aging, is only one of several which women poets are remaking. The remaking is often done under difficult circumstances and often consists in marking a text from which she was erased or where she was fixed and silenced. And yet she must try to balance the elements of innovation and justice, as other poets did before her. Even if she is unclear, unsettled, uncertain. As indeed I was. And may still be.

Ideology is unambiguous; poetry is not. As a younger poet I had discovered that feminism had wonderful strengths as a critique and almost none as an aesthetic. Had I followed the clear line of feminism, which had so sustained me in other ways, I would have found poems which fused the sexual and erotic either oppressive or disaffecting. And I did not. On the contrary, I found many of them beautiful and persuasive. It added both complexity and enrichment that these poems which I needed to reconsider as a woman had shaped and delighted me as a poet.

The contradictions did not stop there. As an Irish poet who was also a woman I had been increasingly aware—at times it was almost a malaise—that Irish women poets had gone from being the objects of the Irish poem to being its authors in a relatively short space of time. It was a rapid and disruptive process. It encountered resistances, some of which were interdictions within the tradition rather than a shortage of permissions outside it. The Irish poetic tradition wove images of women into images of the nation, simplifying both in the process. I had struggled with it and defined myself against it. But this iconography of the Irish poem was a local ordinance. The fusion of the sexual and the erotic was not; it appeared as a customary and enduring feature of poetry rather than of a single place or tradition.

Then why did I not find it still more oppressive? The reason was complex and ambiguous. The more I thought about it, the more the poetic relation between the erotic and sexual seemed to play out a drama of expression rather than a drama of desire. It was a relation between the expressive and the silenced, between the subject and the object. As such it could not just have an aesthetic dimension; it had an ethical one as well. But the ethical dimension—unlike the intercutting of feminine and national in the Irish poem—was extraordinarily complex. The erotic and sexual met in the poem of the tradition in the very place where poetry canvassed one of its great themes: the fracture of sense and spirit. I found it extraordinarily hard to be sure at times whether that beautiful appropriation of the erotic by the sexual, and both by the expressive, was an act of healing or an exercise of power. As I read the poems of the tradition, it could often seem to me that I was entering a beautiful and perilous world filled with my own silence, where I was accorded the unfree status of an object. And yet there was paradox. As I struggled to become my own subject—in poems I could hardly write and in a literary tradition which blurred the feminine and the national— these poems were enabling and illuminating. As a woman I felt some mute and anxious kinship with those erotic objects which were appropriated; as a poet I felt confirmed by the very powers of expression which appropriated them.

IX.

It is a February night. The suburb is dark, and rain is spilling noisily from our gutter onto the garage roof. The garden is black and soaking. The streetlamps are on. My children are teenagers now. Their shoes, clothes, letters and diaries litter every room in the house.

That moment has come to me which was prophesied by another woman's body in a summer twilight years ago. I am older, less hopeful, more accquainted with the craft, more instructed by my failures in it. And once again there is a notebook open on the table by the window. The window looks out to dark roofs and the dripping twigs of the laburnum and the shapes of the garden. If I stood in that garden and looked southwest, I would see the Dublin hills. If I looked east, I would see the suburbs that led to the city. And high in those hills is the river which had made the city: the Liffey, now being refilled by rain. Its source and mouth, its definition and loss seem to me at that moment close to the realizations and dissolutions my body has known in this very house. I walk to the table. I sit down and take up my pen. I begin to write about a river and a woman, about the destiny of water and my sense of growing older. The page fills easily and quickly.

10.

THE WOMAN POET:
HER DILEMMA

I believe that the woman poet today inherits a dilemma. That she does so inevitably, no matter what cause she espouses and whatever ideology she advocates or shuns. That when she sits down to work, when she moves away from her work, when she tries to be what she is struggling to express, at all these moments the dilemma is present, waiting and inescapable.

The dilemma I speak of is inherent in a shadowy but real convergence between new experience and an established aesthetic. What this means in practical terms is that the woman poet today is caught in a field of force. Powerful, persuasive voices are in her ear as she writes. Distorting and simplifying ideas of womanhood and poetry fall as shadows between her and the courage of her own experience. If she listens to these voices, yields to these ideas, her work will be obstructed. If, however, she evades the issue, runs for cover and pretends there is there is no pressure, then she is likely to lose the resolution she needs to encompass the critical distance between writing poems and being a poet. A distance which for women is fraught in any case, as I hope to show, with psychosexual fear and doubt.

Dramatize, dramatize, said Henry James. And so I will. Imagine, then, that a woman is going into the garden. She is youngish; her apron is on, and there is flour on her hands. It is early afternoon. She is going there to lift a child who for the third time is about to put laburnum pods into its mouth. This is what she does. But what I have omitted to say in this small sketch is that the woman is a poet. And once she is in the garden, once the child, hot and small and needy, is in her arms, once the frills of shadow around the laburnum and the freakish gold light from it are in her eyes, then her poetic sense is awakened. She comes back through the garden door. She cleans her hands, takes off her apron, sets her child down for an afternoon sleep. Then she sits down to work.

Now it begins. The first of these powerful, distracting voices comes to her. For argument's sake, I will call it the Romantic Heresy. It comes to her as a whisper, an insinuation. What she wants to do is write about the laburnum, the heat of the child, common human love—the mesh of these things. But where, says the voice in her ear, is the interest in all this? How are you going to write a poem out of these plain Janes, these snips and threads of an ordinary day? Now, the voice continues, listen to me, and I will show you how to make all this poetic. A shade here, a nuance there, a degree of distance, a lilt of complaint, and all will be well. The woman hesitates. Suddenly the moment that seemed to her potent and emblematic and true appears commonplace, beyond the pale of art. She is shaken. And there I will leave her, with her doubts and fears, so as to look more closely at what it is that has come between her and the courage of that moment.

♦ ♦ ♦

The Romantic Heresy, as I have chosen to call it, is not romanticism proper, although it is related to it. "Before Wordsworth," writes Lionel Trilling, "poetry had a subject. After Wordsworth its prevalent subject was the poet's own subjectivity." This shift in perception was responsible for much that was fresh and revitalizing in nineteenth-century poetry. Bit it was also responsible for the declension of poetry into self-consciousness, self-invention.

This type of debased romanticism is rooted in a powerful, subliminal suggestion that poets are distinctive not so much because they write poetry as because in order to do so, they have poetic feelings about poetic experiences. That there is a category of experience and expression which is poetic and

all the rest is ordinary and therefore inadmissible. In this way
a damaging division is made between the perception of what
is poetic on the one hand and, on the other, what is merely
human. Out of this emerges the aesthetic which suggests that
in order to convert the second into the first, you must romanticize it. This idea gradually became an article of faith in nineteenth-century postromantic English poetry. When Matthew
Arnold said at Oxford, "the strongest part of our religion is its
unconscious poetry," he was blurring a fine line. He was
himself one of the initiators of a sequence of propositions by
which the poetry of religion became the religion of poetry.

There are obvious pitfalls in all of this for any poet. But
the dangers for a woman poet in particular must be immediately obvious. Women are a minority within the expressive
poetic tradition. Much of their actual experience lacks even
the most rudimentary poetic precedent. "No poet," says
Eliot, "no artist of any kind has his complete meaning alone."
The woman poet is more alone with her meaning than most.
The ordinary routine day that many women live—must
live—to take just one instance, does not figure largely in poetry. Nor the feelings that go with it. The temptations are
considerable, therefore, for a woman poet to romanticize
these routines and these feelings so as to align them with what
is considered poetic.

Now let us go back to the woman at her desk. Let us
suppose that she has recovered her nerve and her purpose.
She remembers what is true: the heat, the fear that her child
will eat the pods. She feels again the womanly power of the

instant. She puts aside the distortions of romanticism. She starts to write again, and once again she is assailed. But this time by another and equally persuasive idea.

And this is feminist ideology or at least one part of it. In recent years feminism has begun to lay powerful prescriptions on writing by women. The most exacting of these comes from that part of feminist thinking which is separatist. Separatist prescriptions demand that women be true to the historical angers which underwrite the women's movement, that they cast aside preexisting literary traditions, that they evolve not only their own writing but the criteria by which to judge it. I think I understand some of these prescriptions. I recognize that they stem from the fact that many feminists—and I partly share the view—perceive a great deal in preexisting literary expression and tradition which is patriarchal, not to say oppressive. I certainly have no wish to be apologetic about the separatist tendency because it offends or threatens or bores—and it does all three—the prevailing male literary establishments. That does not concern me for a moment. There is still prejudice—the Irish poetic community is among the most chauvinist—but as it happens, that is not part of this equation.

What does concern me is that the gradual emphasis on the appropriate subject matter and the correct feelings has become as constricting and corrupt within feminism as within romanticism. In the grip of romanticism and its distortions, women can be argued out of the truth of their feelings, can be marginalized, simplified and devalued by what is, after all, a patriarchal tendency. But does the separatist prescription offer more? I have to say—painful as it may be to dissent from one section of a movement I cherish—that I see no redemption whatsoever in moving from one simplification to the other.

So here again is the woman at her desk. Let us say she is feminist. What is she to make of the suggestion by a poet like Adrienne Rich that "to be a female human being, trying to fulfill female functions in a traditional way, is in direct conflict with the subversive function of the imagination?"

Yet the woman knows that whether or not going into the garden and lifting her child are part of the "traditional way," they have also been an agent and instrument of subversive poetic perception. What is she to do? Should she contrive an anger, invent a disaffection? How is she to separate one obligation from the other, one truth from the other? And what is she to make of the same writer's statement that "to the eye of the feminist, the work of Western male poets now writing reveals a deep, fatalistic pessimism as to the possibilities of change . . . and a new tide of phallocentric sadism." It is no good to say she need not read these remarks. Adrienne Rich is a wonderful poet and her essay—"When We Dead Awaken"—from which these statements are quoted is a central statement in contemporary poetry. It should be read by every poet. So there is no escape. The force or power of this stance, which I would call separatist, but may more accurately be called antitraditional, must be confronted.

Separatist thinking is a persuasive and dangerous influence on any woman poet writing today. It tempts her to disregard the whole poetic past as patriarchal betrayal. It pleads with her to discard the complexities of true feeling for the relative simplicity of anger. It promises to ease her technical problems with the solvent of polemic. It whispers to her that to be feminine in poetry is easier, quicker and more eloquent than the infinitely more difficult task of being human. Above all, it encourages her to feminize her perceptions rather than humanize her femininity.

But women have a birthright in poetry. I believe, though an antitraditional poet might not agree, that when a woman poet begins to write, she very quickly becomes conscious of the silences which have preceded her, which still surround her. These silences will become an indefinable part of her purpose as a poet. Yet as a working poet she will also— if she is honest—recognize that these silences have been at least partly redeemed within the past expressions of other poets, most of them male. And these expressions also will become part of her purpose. But for that to happen, she must have the fullest possible dialogue with them. She needs it; she is entitled to it. And in order to have that dialogue, she must have the fullest dialogue also with her own experience, her own present as a poet. I do not believe that separatism allows for this.

Very well. Let us say that after all this inner turmoil the woman is still writing. That she has taken her courage with both hands and has resisted the prescriptions both of romanticism and separatism. Yet for all that, something is still not right. Once again she hesitates. But why? "Outwardly," says Virginia Woolf, "what is simpler than to write books? Out-

245

wardly what obstacles are there for a woman rather than for a man? Inwardly I think the case is very different. She still has many ghosts to fight, many prejudices to overcome." Ghosts and prejudices. Maybe it is time we took a look at these.

II.

I am going to move away from the exploratory and theoretical into something more practical. Let us say, for argument's sake, that it is a wet Novemberish day in a country town in Ireland. Now, for the sake of going a bit further, let us say that a workshop or the makings of one have gathered in an upstairs room in a school perhaps or an adult education center. The surroundings will—they always are on these occasions—be just a bit surreal. There will be old metal furniture, solid oak tables, the surprising gleam of a new video in the corner. And finally, let us say that among these women gathered here is a woman called Judith. I will call her that a nod in the direction of Virginia Woolf's great essay *A Room of One's Own.* And when I—for it is I who am leading the workshop—get off the train or out of the car and climb the stairs and enter that room, it is Judith—her poems already in her hand—who catches my eye and holds my attention.

"History," says Butterfield, "is not the study of origins; rather it is the analysis of all the mediations by which the past has turned into our present." As I walk into that room, as Judith hands me her poems, our past becomes for a moment a single present. I may know, she may acknowledge, that she will never publish, never evolve. But equally I know we have been in the same place and have inherited the same dilemma.

She will show me her work diffidently. It will lack almost any technical finish—lineation is almost always the chief problem—but that will not concern me in the least. What will concern me, will continue to haunt me, is that it will be saying to me—not verbally but articulately nonetheless—I write poetry, but I am not a poet. And I will realize, without too much being said, that the distance between writing poetry and being a poet is one that she has found in her life and her time just too difficult, too far and too dangerous to travel. I will also feel—whether or not I am being just in the matter— that the distance will have been more impassable for her than for any male poet of her generation. Because it is a preordained distance, composed of what Butterfield might call the unmediated past. On the surface that distance seems to be made up of details: lack of money, lack of like minds and so on. But this is deceptive. In essence the distance is psychosexual, made so by a profound fracture between her sense of the obligations of her womanhood and the shadowy demands of her gift.

In his essay on Juana de Asbaje, Robert Graves sets out to define that fracture. "Though the burden of poetry," he writes, "is difficult enough for a man to bear, he can always humble himself before an incarnate Muse and seek instruction from her. . . . The case of a woman poet is a thousand times worse: since she is herself the Muse, a Goddess without an external power to guide or comfort her, and if she strays even a finger's breadth from the path of divine instinct, must take a violent self-vengeance.''

I may think there is a certain melodrama in Graves's commentary. Yet in a subterranean way this is exactly what women fear. That the role of poet, added to that of woman, may well involve them in unacceptable conflict. The outcome of that fear is constant psychosexual pressure. And the result of that pressure is a final reluctance to have the courage of her own experience. All of which adds up to that distance between writing poems and being a poet, a distance which Judith—even as she hands me her work—is telling me she cannot and must not travel.

I will leave that room angered and convinced. Every poet carries within them a silent constituency, made of suffering and failed expression. Judith and the "compound ghost" that she is—for she is, of course, an amalgam of many women—is mine. It is difficult, if not impossible, to explain to men who are poets—writing as they are with centuries of expression behind them—how emblematic are the unexpressed lives of other women to the woman poet, how intimately they are her own. And how, in many ways, that silence is as much part of her tradition as the troubadours are of theirs. "You who maintain that some animals sob sorrowfully, that the dead have dreams," writes Rimbaud, "try to tell the story of my downfall and my slumber. I no longer know how to speak."

How to speak. I believe that if a woman poet survives, if

she sets out on that distance and arrives at the other end, then she has an obligation to tell as much as she knows of the ghosts within her, for they make up, in essence, her story as well. And that is what I intend to do now.

III.

I began writing poetry in the Dublin of the early sixties. Perhaps *began* is not the right word. I had been there or there-abouts for years: scribbling poems in boarding school, reading Yeats after lights out, reveling in the poetry on the course.

Then I left school and went to Trinity. Dublin was a coherent space then, a small circumference in which to be and become a poet. A single bus journey took you into college for the day. Twilights over Stephen's Green were breath-able and lilac-colored. Coffee beans turned and gritted off the blades in the windows of Roberts' and Bewleys. A single cup of it, moreover, cost ninepence in old money and could be spun out for hours of conversation. The last European city. The last literary smallholding.

Or maybe not. "Until we can understand the assump-tions in which we are drenched," writes Adrienne Rich, "we cannot know ourselves." I entered that city and that climate knowing neither myself nor the assumptions around me. And into the bargain, I was priggish, callow, enchanted by the powers of the intellect.

If I had been less of any of these things, I might have looked about me more. I might have taken note of my sur-roundings. If history is the fable agreed upon, then literary

249

traditions are surely the agreed fiction. Things are put in and left out, are preselected and can be manipulated. If I had looked closely, I might have seen some of the omissions. Among other things, I might have noticed that there were no women poets, old or young, past or present in my immediate environment. Sylvia Plath, it is true, detonated in my consciousness, but not until years later. Adrienne Rich was to follow, and Bishop later still. As it was, I accepted what I found almost without question. And soon enough, without realizing it, without inquiring into it, I had inherited more than a set of assumptions. I had inherited a poem.

This poem was a mixture really, a hybrid of the Irish lyric and the British movement piece. It had identifiable moving parts. It usually rhymed, was almost always stanzaic, had a beginning, middle and end. The relation of music to image, of metaphor to idea was safe, repetitive and derivative. "Ladies, I am tame, you may stroke me," said Samuel Johnson to assorted fashionable women. If this poem could have spoken, it might have said something of the sort. I suppose it was no worse, if certainly no better, than the model most young poets have thrust upon them. The American workshop poem at the moment is just as pervasive and probably no more encouraging of scrutiny. Perhaps this was a bit more anodyne; the "bien-fait poem," as it has since been called; the well-made compromise.

This, then, was the poem I learned to write, labored to write. I will not say it was a damaging model because it was a patriarchal poem. As it happens, it was, but that matters less than that I had derived it from my surroundings, not from my life. It was not my own. That was the main thing. "Almost any young gentleman with a sweet tooth," writes Jane Carlyle of Keats's "Isabella," "might be expected to write such things." The comment is apt.

In due course I married, moved out of the city and into the suburbs—I am telescoping several years here—and had a baby daughter. In so doing, I had, without realizing it, altered my whole situation.

When a woman writer leaves the center of a society, becomes a wife, mother and housewife, she ceases automatically to be a member of that dominant class which she belonged to when she was visible chiefly as a writer. As a student, perhaps, or otherwise as an apprentice. Whatever her writing abilities, henceforth she ceases to be defined by them and becomes defined instead by subsidiary female roles. Jean Baker Miller, an American psychoanalyst, has written about the relegation to women of certain attitudes which a society is uneasy with. "Women," she says, "become the carriers for society of certain aspects of the total human experience, those aspects which remain unsolved." Suddenly, in my early thirties, I found myself a "carrier" of these unsolved areas of experience. Yet I was still a writer, still a poet. Obviously something had to give.

What gave, of course, was the aesthetic. The poem I had been writing no longer seemed necessary or true. On rainy winter afternoons, with the dusk drawn in, the fire lighted and a child asleep upstairs, I felt assailed and renewed by contradictions. I could have said, with Éluard, "there is another world, but it is in this one." To a degree I felt that, yet I hesitated. "That story I cannot write," says Conrad, "weaves itself into all I see, into all I speak, into all I think." So it was with me. And yet I remained uncertain of my ground.

On the one hand, poetic convention—conventions, moreover, which I had breathed in as a young poet—whispered to me that the daily things I did, things which seemed to me important and human, were not fit material for poetry. That is, they were not sanctioned by poetic tradition. But, the whisper went on, they could become so. If I wished to integrate these devalued areas into my poetry, I had only to change them slightly. And so on. And in my other ear, feminist ideology—to which I have never been immune—argued that the life I lived was fit subject for anger and the anger itself the proper subject for poetry.

Yet in my mind and in the work I was starting to do a completely different and opposed conviction was growing: that I stood at the center of the lyric moment itself, in a mesh of colors, sensualities and emotions that were equidistant from poetic convention and political feeling alike. Technically and aesthetically I became convinced that if I could only detach the lyric mode from traditional romantic elitism and the new feminist angers, then I would be able at last to express that moment.

The precedents for this were in painting rather than poetry. Poetry offered spiritual consolation but not technical ex-

ample. In the genre painters of the French eighteenth century—in Jean Baptiste Chardin in particular—I saw what I
was looking for. Chardin's paintings were ordinary in the accepted sense of the word. They were unglamorous, worka-
day, authentic. Yet in his work these objects were not merely
described; they were revealed. The hare in its muslin bag, the
crusty loaf, the woman fixed between menial tasks and
human dreams—these stood out, a commanding text. And I
was drawn to that text. Romanticism in the nineteenth century, it seemed to me, had prescribed that beauty be commended as truth. Chardin had done something different. He
had taken truth and revealed its beauty.

From painting I learned something else of infinite value
to me. Most young poets have bad working habits. They
write their poems in fits and starts, by feast or famine. But
painters follow the light. They wait for it and do their work
by it. They combine artisan practicality with vision. In a
house with small children, with no time to waste, I gradually
reformed my working habits. I learned that if I could not
write a poem, I could make an image, and if I could not make
an image, I could take out a word, savor it and store it.

I have gone into all this because to a certain extent, the
personal witness of a woman poet is still a necessary part of the
evolving criteria by which women and their poetry must be
evaluated. Nor do I wish to imply that I solved my dilemma.
The dilemma persists; the crosscurrents continue. What I
wished most ardently for myself at a certain stage of my work

was that I might find my voice where I had found my vision. I still think this is what matters most and is threatened most for the woman poet.

I am neither a separatist nor a postfeminist. I believe that the past matters, yet I do not believe we will reach the future without living through the womanly angers which shadow this present. What worries me most is that women poets may lose their touch, may shake off their opportunities because of the pressures and temptations of their present position.

It seems to me, at this particular time, that women have a destiny in the form. Not because they are women; it is not as simple as that. Our suffering, our involvement in the collective silence do not—and will never—of themselves guarantee our achievement as poets. But if we set out in the light of that knowledge and that history, determined to tell the human and poetic truth, and if we avoid simplification and self-deception, then I believe we are better equipped than most to discover the deepest possibilities and subversions within poetry itself. Artistic forms are not static. Nor are they radicalized by aesthetes and intellectuals. They are changed, shifted, detonated into deeper patterns only by the sufferings and self-deceptions of those who use them. By this equation, women should break down barriers in poetry in the same way that poetry will break the silence of women. In the process it is important not to mistake the easy answer for the long haul.